More Music That Teaches Spanish!
¡Más música que enseña español!

Original Songs
Illustrations
Creative Activities
by **Patti Lozano**

Dolo Publications, Inc.

Copyright © Patti Lozano 1996
All Rights Reserved
First Printing 1996
Second Printing 1998
Third Printing 2008
Printed in the United States of America
ISBN 978-0-9650980-1-4

This publication is protected by Copyright and permission should be obtained from the publisher prior to any prohibited reproduction, storage in a retrieval system, or transmission in any form or by any means, electronic, mechanical, photocopying, recording or otherwise. Permission for duplication, however, is granted to the individual teacher for any portions of the book that will benefit the student in his/her classroom.

Dolo Publications, Inc.
18315 Spruce Creek Drive
Houston, Texas 77084
Toll Free: 1-800-830-1460
fax: (281)679-9092 or (281)463-4808
Email: orders@dololanguages.com or plozano@sbcglobal.net
www.dololanguages.com

Acknowledgment

I am very indebted to several wonderful individuals whose support, insights, talents and advice have made this songbook possible.

Thank you to my husband, Alberto, who is always willing to listen to song and lyric snippets at the most inopportune times and places, and who then offers wonderful suggestions and solutions. Also thanks to my son, Ari, for singing the part of the little elephant.

Thank you to my mother, Renate Donovan, who believes I can do anything, and makes me believe it also. Working together is a lot of fun.

Thank you to Bob Vestiwig, who loves creating music as much as I do, and can make his guitar sing in any style. I can't thank him enough for his friendship, musicianship and time.

And thank you to my other dear friends and fellow musicians — Roy Cavazos (percussion, saxophone, vocals), Bob Meinecke (vocals), Judy Ridenour (accordion), Nancy Rovenstine (piano and vocals), Glenda Waugh (vocals) and Cindy Angel (flute). These people generously donated their time, creativity, spirit and skill to create the *"More Music That Teaches Spanish!"* CD. They made my songs come alive!

Patti Lozano

Other works by Patti Lozano
(Published by Dolo Publications, Inc.)

Music That Teaches Spanish!
Leyendas con canciones
Mighty Mini-Plays for the Spanish Classroom
Mighty Mini-Plays for the French Classroom
Mighty Mini-Plays for the German Classroom
Mighty Mini-Plays for the ESL Classroom
Music That Teaches French!
Music That Teaches German!
Music That Teaches English!
Get Them Talking!
Spanish Grammar Swings!
Teatro de Cuentos de Hadas
Latin American Legends: on Page, on Stage and in Song
Skinny Skits (in Spanish)
Petites Pièces de Théâtre

Contents

I. Introduction — i – iv

II. Identification of Target Vocabulary on Vocabulary Cards — v – vi

III. Songs, Games and Activities, Lyrics, Templates and Vocabulary Cards

1. Voy al centro *(downtown: buildings and city)* — **1a, b, c, d, e**
2. Mi libro perdido *(rooms in the house)* — **2a, b, c, d, e, f, g**
3. Las siete iguanas *(descriptive adjectives, superlatives)* — **3a, b, c, d**
4. El rancho de Pancho *(farm and domestic animals)* — **4a, b, c, d, e**
5. Soy un pajarito *(prepositions)* — **5a, b, c, d**
6. Derecha, izquierda y alrededor *(directions, preposition review)* — **6a, b, c, d, e**
7. Quiero viajar en un coche azul *(transportation and adjectives)* — **7a, b, c, d, e**
8. Cáscara de coco, jugo de piña *(sea animals)* — **8a, b, c, d**
9. ¡Vamos a cantar! (Yo canto, tú cantas) — **9a, b, c, d**
   (present tense verb forms; 1st & 2nd person singular only)
10. Yo prefiero México *(topographical terms)* — **10a, b, c, d**
11. Leonor, mi amor, por favor *(personal hygiene and commands)* — **11a, b, c, d**
12. Dos elefantes — **12a, b, c, d, e**
    (leisure activities, the verb "querer" 1st & 2nd person sing. only)
13. O águila, escúchame *(nature, countryside)* — **13a, b, c, d**
14. Hay que ir al zoológico *(zoo animals, countries)* — **14a, b, c, d, e**

IV. Glossary (Spanish–English) — 15

V. Guidelines for Spanish Pronounciation — 23

VI. Order page — 25

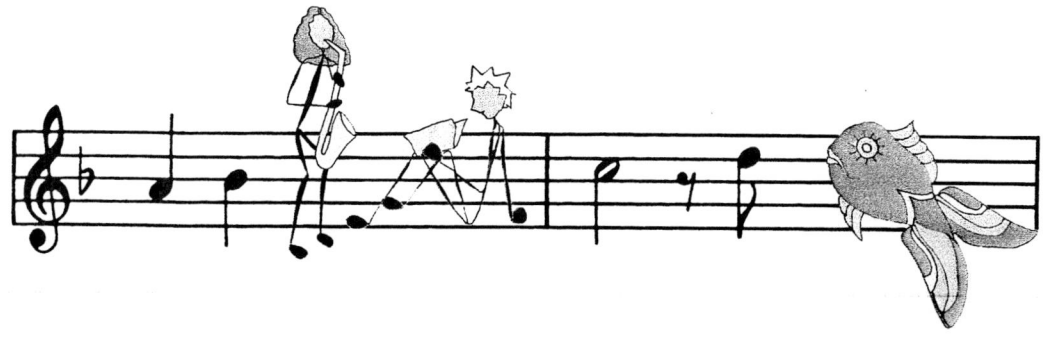

Introduction

More Music That Teaches Spanish! was written as a result of the successful introduction and implementation of the first volume, **Music That Teaches Spanish!** It is a comprehensive song and activity book for beginning and intermediate learners of Spanish. The fourteen songs within reinforce basic topics and structures in a fun and creative manner. Language objectives presented in musical format makes language learning effortless and memorable for students of any age. As students sing the songs in **More Music That Teaches Spanish!** they will:

- learn useful vocabulary in entertaining context
- discover meaning through illustrations
- take part in creative activities to augment learning and encourage speaking
- play games and drills to reinforce retention

Although the text is directed primarily towards elementary and middle schools, the songs are enjoyable for students of all levels and ages. They may be heard on the accompanying audio-CD. The tunes comprise many musical styles such as the rock 'n roll 50's, the folk sounds of the Andes, blues, bluegrass and, of course, the vibrant rhythms of Latin America.

All song and activity pages are designed as blackline masters and, in fact, are printed on only one side of the paper in order to facilitate duplication. *The audio-CD may not be reproduced.*

Each song and rhyme meets one or more teaching objectives found in most beginning and intermediate Spanish textbooks. Topics begin where **Music That Teaches Spanish!** left off: going to the city, adjectives, prepositions, directions, transportation, the beginning of conjugation, topography, hygiene and commands. There are also four animal-related songs; farm animals, sea animals, countryside animals and zoo animals. The song lyrics, while more complex than in the first volume, are still uncomplicated and the tunes are simple, but catchy and never "babyish." The Contents Page contains a brief description of the topic emphasized in each song.

Once students are comfortable with the melodies and lyrics they may want to improvise their own original verses to manipulate their newfound vocabulary. An additional CD entitled **Just Music!** is available (see the Order Page in the back of the book) which enables classes to do just that. The CD contains the music tracks minus the vocals to 9 of the songs in **Music That Teaches Spanish!** and 6 of the songs in *More Music That Teaches Spanish!*

Author and composer, Patti Lozano, has taught both elementary and middle school Spanish and music. She created the songs in **Music That Teaches Spanish!** and **More Music That Teaches Spanish!** for a 1st through 5th grade instructional video series filmed in Houston and implemented in school districts throughout Texas. Mrs. Lozano writes with love and understanding for young people who are trying to learn a new language. She firmly believes that singing and chanting are powerful tools that effortlessly enhance language acquisition at all levels of instruction. Mrs. Lozano now sings her songs with Spanish students around the country. When she meets a group of students, feet begin to tap, hands clap, bodies sway with the music, faces smile, voices ring out... and, most important, children are singing, thinking and speaking Spanish!

Book Format

This song and activity book has been designed to be "teacher-friendly." Each song contains pages that follow an **"a, b, c, d"** (and often an **"e, f and g"**) format:

- **The "a" page** displays the song in traditional musical notation with guitar chords. This page enables teachers who play the piano, guitar or autoharp to accompany their students. Students who play band instruments may want a copy of this page. Spanish lyrics and their English translations (literal, not singable) to all verses are found here.

- **The "b" page** is the teacher's lesson guide and teaching suggestion portion of the book. Please note that the "b" page is always double-sided! The "b" page topics include:

    1. *Language Objectives:* A text box encloses both vocabulary and structural objectives for this song. Examples are given and all targeted vocabulary is listed.

    2. *Extension Games and Activities:* A variety of innovative learning activities are suggested and described to reinforce the vocabulary and structures highlighted in each song. The games are often related to the activity templates and flash cards on corresponding **"d, e,"** and occasional **"f"** and **"g"** pages.

    3. *Make it Meaningful:* This section highlights an activity that relates the target vocabulary and structures to the student's life and interests outside the classroom.

    4. *The Song as a Teaching Tool:* This section offers ideas for enhancing and extending the targeted vocabulary and structures via modification of the song. There are suggestions for improvisation, role-play, composition, choreography and much more.

- **The "c" page** is the illustrated song, and is for the students. All song lyrics are illustrated, and typed in a larger font, so that students and teachers can follow the content of the song by recognizing the vocabulary via drawings. Duplicate this page so that all students have a sheet. If every **"c"** page in the book is copied, then each student will have a personally illustrated songbook! Teachers may also choose to enlarge this page as a transparency to use as a visual aid.

- **The "d, e, f" and "g" pages** contain all template and activity flash cards necessary to play the creative, open-ended, interactive games and activities suggested on the **"b"** pages. There are vocabulary cards, game boards, poems to choreograph, and much more. The combination of singing and hands-on manipulatives is a team that can't be beat for joyful learning and retention of vocabulary and structures!

Why does music "teach" so well?

First and foremost, kids love to sing. Melodies breathe life into drills. The most boring equation in the world becomes vibrantly alive when set to a melody.

Kids don't learn much by listening. They learn by doing, by interacting. And singing is definitely interactive. Add clapping, bouncing, gesturing, choreography, tapping and the tunes and lyrics work their way into the learner's muscles where they will remain forever. Singing is the ultimate device to achieve 100% retention of the target material... forever!

Lately much research has been conducted about multiple intelligences inherent in all human beings, by such experts in the profession as Howard Gardner, David G. Lazear and Eric Jensen. Music and rhythm rank high among the seven intelligences described below. And the act of singing itself contains fragments of most of the other identified intelligences!

- **Verbal/Linguistic** - Relating to words and language, both written and spoken

- **Logical/Mathematical** - Dealing with thinking, reasoning, numbers, and recognition of abstract patterns

- **Visual/Spatial** - Thinking and visualizing images and pictures

- **Music/Rhythmic** - recognizing tonal patterns and environmental sounds; learning through rhyme, rhythm, and beats

- **Body/Kinesthetic** - Relating to physical movement; includes the brain's motor cortex which controls bodily motion

- **Intrapersonal** - Learning through self-reflection and liking to work alone

- **Interpersonal** - Learning through person-to-person, group relationships, and communication

A brief look at successful second language teaching strategies

The activities listed below have proven successful in classrooms where music is an integral part of the curriculum.

◆ **TPR (Total Physical Response)** — consists of simple commands given by the teacher and followed by the students. The pattern is as follows:
    a) the teacher models the command without expecting a response from the students
    b) the students respond to the command as a group
    c) commands are given to individual students by the teacher
    d) the students give the commands to each other

This method is an effective way to introduce all target vocabulary depicted on the page "d" flashcard. Song #16, for example, *"Jugo de naranja,"* focuses on foods. After singing the song and becoming familiar with the target vocabulary words, the teacher distributes sets of the food flashcards (16d) to all students. The teacher then states, *"Toca el jugo de naranja."* Without a word, students touch their orange juice flashcards and then wait for the next command. The commands can become more fun and creative as more vocabulary is added. Some of the most useful commands are listed in the box below.

Muéstrame...	*(Show me...)*	Examples:	*"Muéstrame la pluma."*
Dame...	*(Give me...)*		*"Dame la hamburguesa."*
Busca ...	*(Look for...)*		*"Busca la camisa."*
Pon...	*(Put...)*		*"Pon la sal en la mesa."*
Toma...	*(Take...)*		*"Toma la silla."*
Anda con...	*(Walk with...)*		*"Anda con el color rojo."*
Corre con...	*(Run with...)*		*"Corre con el pelo."*
Párate con...	*(Stand up with...)*		*"Párate con el plátano."*
Siéntate con...	*(Sit down with...)*		*"Siéntate con 'Tengo frío."*

◆ **Role-playing** — in large groups, pairs or alone. Some songs, such as *"Leonor, mi amor, por favor"* (Song #11) encourage role-playing the entire story within the song.

◆ **Creating new verses** — and using diverse or extended vocabulary. For example, *"Cáscara de coco, jugo de piña"* (Song #8) can add endless verses with additional animals and their activities.

◆ **Poster-size songs** — any song ("c" pages) can be enlarged via transparency so that students can follow the lyrics more closely. One student can "chart" the lyrics with a pointer for the class. Do this only after the song has been learned orally!

◆ **Play games**—lots of them! Always introduce new material quickly, and then move on to the games, because that's where students perk up and really try! A favorite game (and a perfect TPR exercise) regardless of age or grade is *"¡Simón dice!"* ("Simon says!")

Identification of Target Vocabulary on Vocabulary Cards ("d, e f" and "g" pages)

1d: el centro *(Downtown)*
  Row 1: el cine *(cinema)*, la biblioteca *(library)*, el supermercado *(supermarket)*
  Row 2: la tienda (de ropa), *(clothing store)*, los edificios *(buildings)*, el hospital *(hospital)*
  Row 3: la oficina de correo *(post office)*, la farmacia *(pharmacy)*, el banco *(bank)*
  Row 4: el hotel *(hotel)*, el museo *(museum)*, el restaurante *(restaurant)*

1e: ¿Qué hay en los edicficios? *(What's in the buildings?)*
  Note: these items are in the same rows as the page 1d buildings to which they belong.
  Row 1: las palomitas *(popcorn)*, el libro *(book)*, el pan *(bread)*
  Row 2: los pantalones *(pants)*, la computadora *(computer)*, el médico *(doctor)*
  Row 3: la carta/el sobre *(letter/envelope)*, la medicina *(medicine)*, el dinero *(money)*
  Row 4: la llave *(key)*, el dinosaurio *(dinosaur)*, la hamburgesa *(hamburger)*

2e: La familia *(Family members)*
  Row 1: la mamá/la madre *(mother)*, el papá/el padre *(father)*, la hermana/la hija *(sister/daughter)*, el hermano/el hijo *(brother/son)*
  Row 2: la abuela *(grandmother)*, el abuelo *(grandfather)*, el perro *(dog)*, el gato *(cat)*

2f: Los cuartos de la casa *(Rooms of the house)*
  Row 1: la sala *(livingroom)*, la cocina *(kitchen)*
  Row 2: el dormitorio *(bedroom)*, el baño *(bathroom)*
  Row 3: el comedor *(dining room)*, la oficina *(office)*
  Row 4: el jardín/el patio *(garden/patio)*, el garaje *(garage)*

2g: ¿Qué hay en los cuartos? *(What's in the rooms?)*
  Row 1: el sofá *(sofa/couch)*, el refrigerador *(refrigerator)*, la cama *(bed)*
  Row 2: la alfombra *(rug/carpet)*, la ducha *(shower bath)*, la mesa *(table)*
  Row 3: la ventana/las cortinas *(window/curtains)*, la lámpara *(lamp)*, la planta *(plant)*
  Row 4: el estante para libros *(bookcase)*, el coche *(car)*, la bicicleta *(bicycle)*

4d: Los animales del rancho y los animales domesticados *(Farm animals and pets)*
  Row 1: el caballo *(horse)*, la vaca *(cow)*, la oveja *(sheep)*
  Row 2: el cerdo/el cochino *(pig)*, el pato *(duck)*, el perro *(dog)*
  Row 3: el pez *(fish)*, la gallina *(hen/live chicken)*, el gato *(cat)*
  Row 4: el perico/el loro *(parrot)*, el ratoncito *(mouse)*, la llama *(llama)*

7d: El transporte *(Transportation)*
  Row 1: el coche *(car)*, el autobús *(bus)*, el avión *(airplane)*
  Row 2: el barco (de vela) *(boat/sailboat)*, la bicicleta *(bicycle)*, el elefante *(elephant)*
  Row 3: el caballo *(horse)*, el globo *(balloon)*, el camión *(truck)*
  Row 4: la motocicleta *(motorcycle)*, el tren *(train)*, de pie *(on foot)*

Identification of Target Vocabulary on Flashcards *(continued)*

8d: **Los animales del mar** *(Sea animals)*
  Row 1: la ballena *(whale)*, el tiburón *(shark)*, la concha *(sea shell)*
  Row 2: el pez *(fish)*, el coral *(coral)*, la medusa *(jellyfish)*
  Row 3: el camarón *(shrimp)*, el delfín *(dolphin)*, la estrella del mar *(starfish)*
  Row 4: la tortuga *(turtle)*, el pulpo *(octopus)*, el cangrejo *(crab)*

8d: **Acciones – los verbos** *(Actions – verbs)*
  Row 1: cantar: yo canto, tú cantas *(to sing: I sing, you sing)*, pintar: yo pinto, tú pintas *(to paint)*, leer: yo leo, tú lees *(to read)*
  Row 2: nadar: yo nado, tú nadas *(to swim)*, hablar: yo hablo, tú hablas *(to speak/ talk)*, caminar: yo camino, tú caminas *(to walk)*
  Row 3: bailar: yo bailo, tú bailas *(to dance)*, mirar: yo miro, tú miras *(to look at)*, jugar: yo juego, tú juegas *(to play a game)*
  Row 4: comer: yo como, tú comes *(to eat)*, beber: yo bebo, tú bebes *(to drink)*, tocar: yo toco, tú tocas *(to touch or to play an instrument)*

12d: **Recreos pasatiempos** *(Leisure-time activities)*
  Row 1: mirar la televisión *(watch television)*: escribir en la computadora *(write on the computer)*, escuchar el radio *(listen to the radio)*
  Row 2: jugar con carritos y muñecas *(play with cars and dolls)*, tocar el piano *(play the piano)*, jugar al béisbol *(play baseball)*
  Row 3: dormir *(sleep)*, ir de compras *(go shopping)*, viajar *(travel)*
  Row 4: ir al cine *(go to the movies)* comer en un restaurante *(eat at a restaurant)*, hablar por teléfono *(talk on the phone)*

13d: **Ir al campo** *(Going to the countryside)*
  Row 1: la águila *(eagle)*, el campo *(countryside/field)*, el conejo *(rabbit)*
  Row 2: la culebra *(snake)*, las hormigas *(ants)*, el puercoespín *(porcupine)*
  Row 3: el árbol *(tree)*, la ardilla *(squirrel)*,
    la rama, las hojas y las flores *(branch, leaves and flowers)*
  Row 4: el venado *(deer)*, el bosque *(forest/woods)*, la mariposa *(butterfly)*

14d: **Los animales del zoológico** *(Zoo animals)*
  Row 1: el tigre *(tiger)*, el oso *(bear)*, el mono/el chango *(monkey)*
  Row 2: el canguro *(kangaroo)*, el perico/el loro *(parrot)*, la foca *(seal)*
  Row 3: el elefante *(elephant)*, el camello *(camel)*, el flamingo/el flamenco *(flamingo)*
  Row 4: el pingüino *(penguin)* el cocodrillo *(crocodile)*, la rana (frog)

Songs and Activity Page Organization

a. Songs with Musical Notation and Guitar Chords, Complete Lyrics and literal English Translations

b. Language Objectives and Examples, Teaching Suggestions including:
   Extension Games and Activities
   Make it Meaningful
   The Song as a Teaching Tool)
   (Page "b" is always double-sided.)

c. Illustrated Songs and Lyrics

d, e, f, g. Vocabulary Cards, Activity Templates, Exercises and Game Boards

1. Voy al centro

Words and Music by Patti Lozano

Cuando estoy aburrida y no sé que hacer	When I'm bored and don't know what to do
No quiero jugar, no quiero trabajar o leer	I don't want to play, don't want to work or read
Yo voy al centro, voy al cine allá	I go downtown, I go to the movies there
Voy al centro, voy a la biblioteca	I go downtown, I go to the library
Voy al centro, voy al supermercado	I go downtown, I go to the grocery store
Voy al centro de la ciudad	I go to the downtown of the city

Cuando estoy aburrida y no sé que hacer	When I'm bored and don't know what to do
No quiero jugar, no quiero trabajar o leer	I don't want to play, don't want to work or read
Yo voy al centro, voy a todas las tiendas	I go downtown, I go to the all of the stores
Voy al centro, voy a las oficinas	I go downtown, I go to the offices
Voy al centro, voy a un restaurante	I go downtown, I go to a restaurant
Voy al centro de la ciudad	I go to the downtown of the city

Cuando estoy aburrida y no sé que hacer	When I'm bored and don't know what to do
No quiero jugar, no quiero trabajar o leer	I don't want to play, don't want to work or read
Yo voy al centro, la calle llena de coches	I go downtown, the street full of cars
Voy al centro, a caminar con la gente	I go downtown, to walk with the people
Voy al centro, donde nunca estoy triste,	I go downtown, where I'm never sad
Voy al centro de la ciudad	I go to the downtown of the city

1. Voy al centro
Teaching Suggestions

Language Objectives: Going Downtown
☺ Vocabulary: **la ciudad** *(city)* **el centro** *(downtown)*
  la calle *(street)* **los coches** *(cars)*

Places in the city: * Items generally found in these places:
  el cine *(movie theater)* **las palomitas** *(popcorn)*
  la biblioteca *(library)* **el libro, los libros** *(book, books)*
  el supermercado *(supermarket)* **el pan** *(bread)*
  la oficina *(office)* **los escritorios, las sillas** *(desks, chairs)*
  la tienda de ropa *(clothing store)* **los pantalones** *(pants, trousers)*
  el restaurante *(restaurant)* **la hamburguesa** *(hamburger)*

*These items correspond to the illustrations on page 1e

☺ Structures: **Voy al centro.**   *I go downtown.*

☺ Extension Vocabulary: (corresponds to the illustrations on pages 1d and 1e.)
  More places in the city: Items found in these places:
  los edificios *(buildings)* **la computadora** *(computer)*
  el banco *(bank)* **el dinero** *(money)*
  el correo *(post office)* **la carta** *(letter)*
  la farmacia *(pharmacy)* **la medicina** *(medicine)*
  el hospital *(hospital)* **el médico** *(doctor)*
  el hotel *(hotel)* **la llave** *(key)*
  el museo *(museum)* **el dinosaurio** *(dinosaur)*

Extension Games and Activities:

A. **¿Qué hay en la bolsa?** *(What's in the purse?)*
   Amazingly enough, most of the items in a woman's purse may be related to one of the target vocabulary establishments! A teacher pulls items out of her purse or briefcase and students identify the location where the item originated. For example:
   Teacher pulls out: Students say it comes from:
   a receipt   *el supermercado, el restaurante, la tienda*
   a dollar bill   *el banco*
   a Kleenex™   *el supermercado, la farmacia*
   lipstick   *la farmacia, el supermercado*

B. **Un sábado perfecto en el centro** *(A perfect Saturday downtown)*
   Ask the students to imagine a perfect Saturday downtown and to write or talk about it. Who do they go with? What is the time table? Where do they go? What do they do? For example:
   "Mi amiga Laura y yo vamos al centro a las 10:00. Vamos a la farmacia. Compro perfume. A las 11:00 vamos al cine. Compro palomitas. A la 1:00 vamos al restaurante. Compro una hamburguesa. A las 3:00 vamos a casa."

C. Use the vocabulary cards on pages 1d and 1e to play the following activities:
   1. Play "**Make a Match**". The teacher holds a set of 1d cards (places), and distributes a set of 1e cards among students. The teacher shows one card to the class and identifies it, (i.e. *"la tienda"*). The student with the matching 1e card stands, shows the card to the class and says, *"Voy a la farmacia. Compro medicina."*
   2. Play "**Concentration**". Pair students and give each pair a full set of 1d (places) and 1e (object) cards. Students shuffle all of the cards together and spread them out face down between them. Students take turns finding matching sets (matching a place with an object), calling out the vocabulary words as they turn the cards over.
   3. Play "**Necesito dinero**". Divide the class in half so that the students are standing against opposite walls, facing each other. Give each student in the right-side group one 1d (places) vocabulary card and instruct them not to show their cards to anyone. Give each student in the left-side group one 1e (object) vocabulary card. The teacher now names an object. The student at the left side with this card must formulate a question, and has three turns to try to locate the establishment she needs to find. For example:
      Teacher: *el médico*
      Student from left side with "el médico" card: (walks to someone in the R side): *Necesito un médico. "¿Hay un médico aquí?"*
      Student from right side group (if he HAS the hospital card) *Sí, este es un hospital. Hay un médico aquí.*
      (Or – if he does NOT have the hospital card) *No, lo siento mucho. Este no es un hospital. Este es un banco. No hay un médico aquí.*
      Continue playing until all students find their matches.

Make it Meaningful

Have each student draw the blueprint of a town, a wing of a mall, or a familiar neighborhood shopping center. Share them. For example;
   "En mi colonia hay una farmacia. Se llama Walgreens. Compro medicina allí.
   Hay un supermercado. Se llama Kroger. Compro plátanos allí.
   Hay una tienda grande. Se llama Kohl's." Compro zapatos allí."

The Song as a Teaching Tool

Research an ASL (American Sign Language) site on the internet. An excellent one that both describes the movement and allows you to see it modeled in real time is Michigan State University's Communication Technology Lab. Find it on the internet at:
http://commtechlab.msu.edu/sites/aslweb/browser.htm
Find the signs for the target vocabulary words and learn to sign them. For example:
aburrido(a) - the forefinger drills a hole into the side of the nose [bored]
sé - the fingertips touch the forehead to indicate that knowledge is in the brain [know]
hacer - the hands twist as if they were putting something together or making something
no - the forefinger and middle finger snap closed on the thumb

Sing the song and sign the vocabulary words in ASL. Students learn two languages for the price of one!

1. Voy al centro

Cuando estoy aburrida y no sé que hacer
No quiero jugar, no quiero trabajar o leer...

Yo voy al centro, voy al cine allá
Voy al centro, voy a la biblioteca
Voy al centro, voy al supermercado
Voy al centro de la ciudad

Cuando estoy aburrida y no sé que hacer
No quiero jugar, no quiero trabajar o leer
Yo voy al centro, voy a todas las tiendas
Voy al centro, voy a las oficinas
Voy al centro, voy a un restaurante
Voy al centro de la ciudad

Cuando estoy aburrida y no sé que hacer
No quiero jugar, no quiero trabajar o leer
Yo voy al centro, la calle llena de coches
Voy al centro, a caminar con la gente
Voy al centro, donde nunca estoy triste
Voy al centro de la ciudad

1. Voy al centro

See page 1b for game and activity ideas using these vocabulary cards.

1. Voy al centro

See page 1b for game and activity ideas using these vocabulary cards.

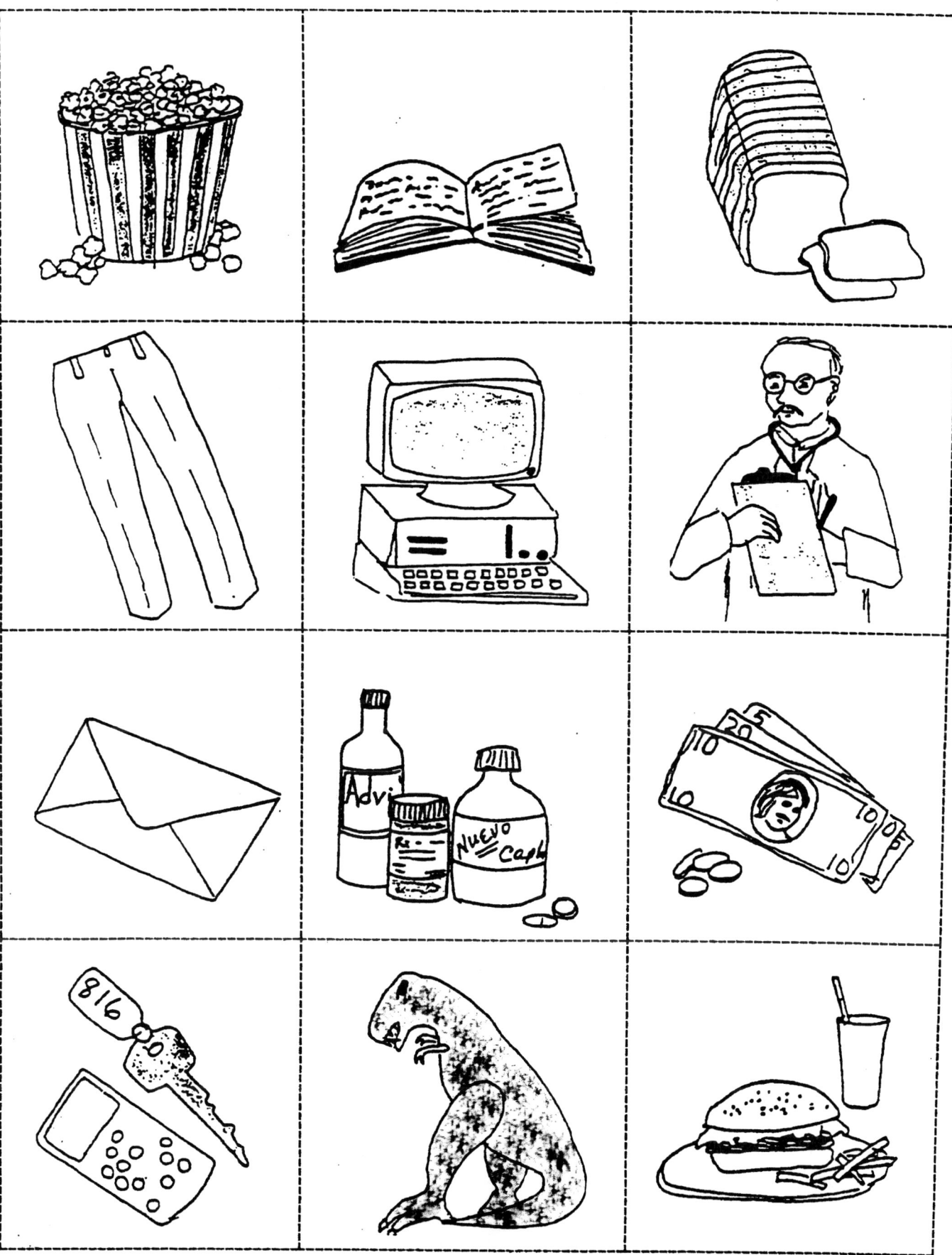

1e

2. Mi libro perdido

Words and music by Patti Lozano

[Sheet music]

Mi libro, mi libro, mi libro está perdido
Mi libro, aunque no es mi favorito
Mi libro, mi libro, lo necesito mucho
Porque no es mi libro, es el libro de mi tío

Estribillo:
   Adentro y afuera me lo buscaré (4X)

1. A veces yo leo mi libro en la sala
   A veces yo leo mi libro en la sala
   A veces yo leo mi libro en la sala
   Aquì en la sala - mi libro buscaré.

2. la cocina
3. el dormitorio

Mi libro, mi libro, ya no está perdido
Mi libro, lo tengo, aunque no estoy contento
Mi libro, mi libro, mi pobrecito libro
Está en el jardìn... lo come mi perrito

My book, my book, my book is lost
My book, although it's not my favorite
My book, my book, I need it a lot
Because it isn't my book, it's my uncle's book

Refrain:
Inside and outside I will look for it (4X)

1. *Sometimes I read my book in the livingroom*
   Sometimes I read my book in the livingroom
   Sometimes I read my book in the livingroom
   Here in the livingroom I will look for my book

2. *the kitchen*
3. *the bedroom*

My book, my book, it's not lost anymore
My book, I have it, although I'm not happy
My book, my book, my poor little book
It's in the garden... my dog is eating it

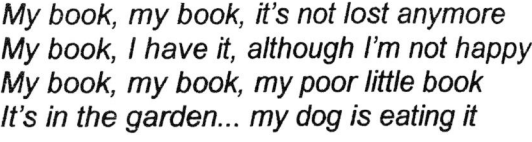

2. Mi libro perdido
Teaching Suggestions

Language Objectives: Rooms in the house
- ☺ Vocabulary: **el libro** *(book)*   **adentro** *(inside)*   **afuera** *(outside)*

  Rooms in the house: *Items generally found in these rooms:
  - **la sala** *(living room)*   **el sofá** *(sofa)*
  - **el dormitorio** *(bedroom)*   **la cama** *(bed)*
  - **la cocina** *(kitchen)*   **el refrigerador** *(refrigerator)*
  - **el jardín, el patio** *(garden, yard)*   **la planta, la maceta** *(plant, flowerpot)*
  -    **la lámpara** *(lamp)*

- ☺ Structures: **a veces**   *sometimes*

  Yo leo mi libro en _____. *(I read my book in _____.)*

- ☺ Extension Vocabulary: (corresponds to the illustrations on pages 1f and 1g)

  More areas of a house: Items found in these areas:
  - **el comedor** *(dining room)*   **la mesa, las sillas** *(table, chairs)*
  - **el baño** *(bathroom)*   **la ducha** *(shower bath)*
  - **el garage** *(garage)*   **la alfombra** *(rug)*
  - **la oficina** *(office)*   **la ventana, las cortinas** *(window, curtains)*
  - **el cuarto de recreo** *(playroom)*   **el estante para libros** *(bookcase)*
  -    **el coche** *(car)*
  -    **la bicicleta** *(bicycle)*

- ☺ Extension Structures:
  - ¿Dónde lees tu libro?   *(Where do you read your book?)*
  - ¿Cuál es tu cuarto favorito? *(Which is your favorite room?)*
  - ¿Cuántos(as) _____ hay en _____? *(How many _____ are there in _____?)*

Extension Games and Activities:

A. **¿Qué hay en la casa?** *(What's in the house?)*

   Make a transparency of page 2d (the cross-section of a house) to display to the students. Ask "*¿Qué hay en la casa?*" The students name as many rooms and items in the house as possible. Then ask the students about their own houses. Ask questions such as:
   - ¿Cuántos dormitorios hay en tu casa? (How many bedrooms are in your house?)
   - ¿Qué hay en tu dormitorio? (What's in your bedroom?)
   - ¿De qué color es tu dormitorio? (What color is your bedroom?)

B. **Uniting family and rooms**

   Make a class set of activity pages 1d (house) and 1e (family members). Distribute a set to each student. Students may color in the people and pets so they may be seen more clearly in the house. Place students in pairs. Instruct each student to place family members and pets in different rooms. Students then take turns describing the set-up to their partners. For example:

   "La mamá está en la sala. El papá está en el baño. La abuela está en el comedor."

★Variation: Students may take turns instructing their partners as to where to place each family member in the house, for example:
"*Pon el hijo en el dormitorio pequeño. Pon el perro en la cocina.*"

C. **Flashcard activities**
   1. **Fill Your Rooms Fast!** Copy and cut a number of 2f (room) and 2g (furnishings) flashcards, making sure to keep them in separate piles. Place each pile of cards into a paper bag and shake the two bags to mix up the cards well. Divide the class into two groups, *"los perros"* and *"los gatos,"* for example. Each *"perro"* chooses three cards from the room bag. Each *"gato"* picks a handful (about 15 cards) from the object bag. Each *"perro"* must fill up his 3 rooms with at least three objects each that are common to that room. They do this by going to various *"gatos"* and saying something like, *"Tengo un dormitorio. Tienes una cama?"* All *"perros"* should try to have their rooms filled with appropriate furnishings within the time limit set by the teacher.

   2. Play **"Duermo en la cocina y mi cama es una maceta"**. (*"I sleep in the kitchen and my bed is a flowerpot."*) Once again, place those cut-up vocabulary cards (pages 2f - rooms and 2g - furnishings) in two paper bags. On the board, write the sentence, *"Duermo en _____ y mi cama es un(a) _____."* Brainstorm the obvious correct choice of words to fill in those blanks. Now everyone is going to have some fun with that sentence. Each student chooses one word from each bag and announces to the class where he/she sleeps and what the bed is. For example, a student might have to say, *"Duermo en el garage y mi cama es una mesa."* Who knows what crazy combinations they'll come up with. Finally, you may have each student choose his favorite combination and draw a picture of it, labeling it with the odd sentence.

Make it Meaningful

La casa de mis sueños (*The House of my Dreams*) Ask students to draw and color their dream houses. They may then show and describe them to the class. Example:
"*Mi casa es grande. Mi casa es azul y roja. Mi casa tiene cinco dormitorios y diez camas. Hay una cocina grande con muchas ventanas. Hay un patio con muchos animales. Hay cuatro baños en mi casa.*"

The Song as a Teaching Tool

Make and sing a **Song Collage**. Have students bring to class magazine pictures of various rooms as well as separate photos of common furnishings and objects found in those rooms. Make two collages on large sheets of cardboard, one being a room collage and the other being a furnishings collage.

Sing the song, changing the word *"leo"* ["I read"] to *"veo"* ["I see"], creating many different verses by combining the items on the two collages. A couple of verses might go like this:
"*A veces yo veo mi zapato en la sala....*"
"*A veces yo veo mi papá en el jardín...*"
"*A veces yo veo mi televisión en el garage...*"

2. Mi libro perdido

Mi libro, mi libro, mi libro está perdido
Mi libro, aunque no es mi favorito
Mi libro, mi libro, lo necesito mucho
Porque no es mi libro; es el libro de mi tío

Estribillo: Adentro y afuera me lo buscaré (4X)

1. A veces yo leo mi libro en la sala
   A veces yo leo mi libro en la sala
   A veces yo leo mi libro en la sala
   Aquí en la sala - mi libro buscaré

2. A veces yo leo mi libro en la cocina
   A veces yo leo mi libro en la cocina
   A veces yo leo mi libro en la cocina
   Aquí en la cocina - mi libro buscaré

4. Mi libro, mi libro, ya no está perdido
   Mi libro, lo tengo, aunque no estoy contento
   Mi libro, mi libro, mi pobrecito libro
   Está en el jardín... ¡lo come mi perrito!

3. A veces yo leo mi libro en el dormitorio...

2. Mi libro perdido

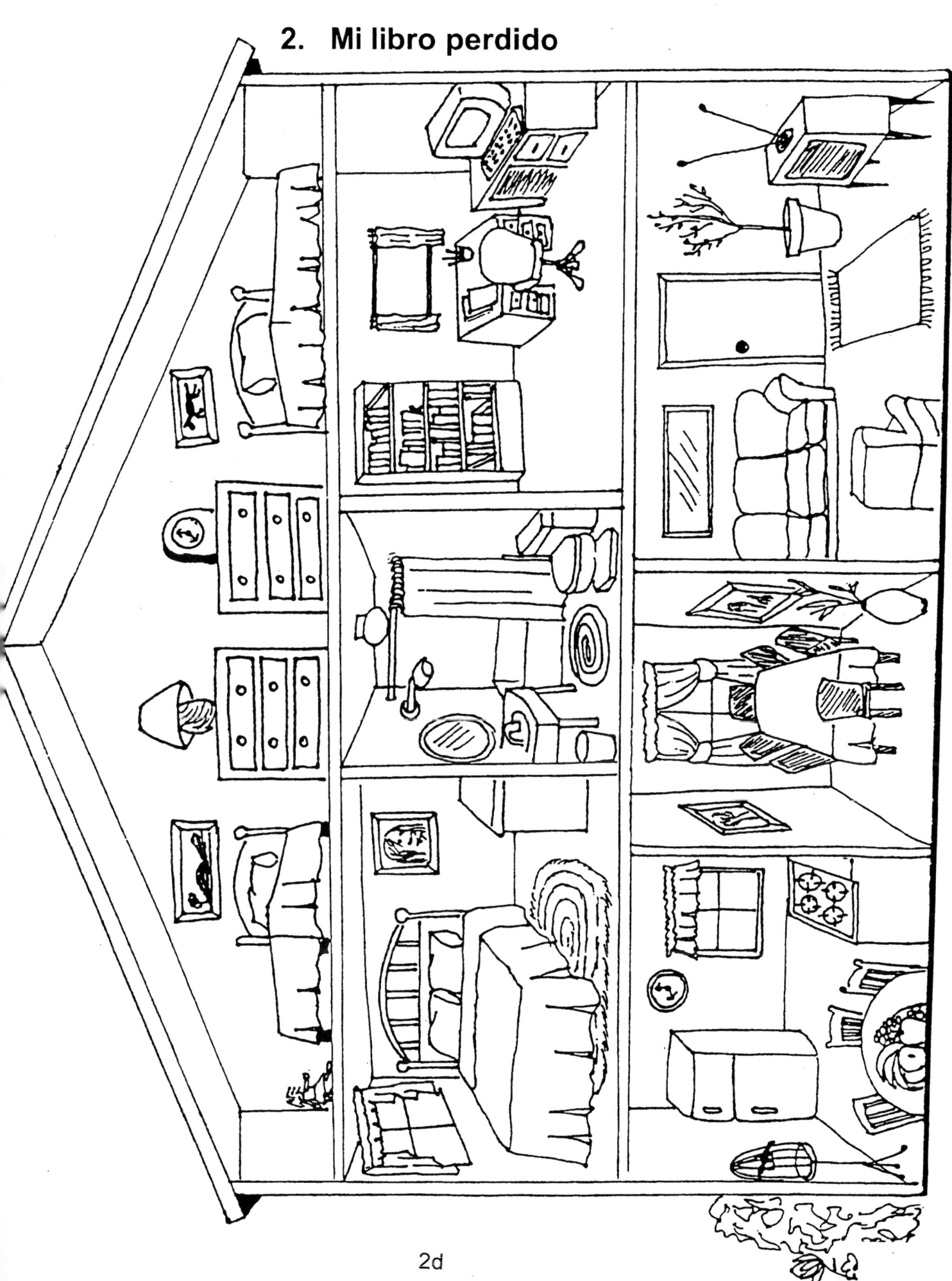

2. Mi libro perdido

See page 2b for game and activity ideas using these vocabulary cards.

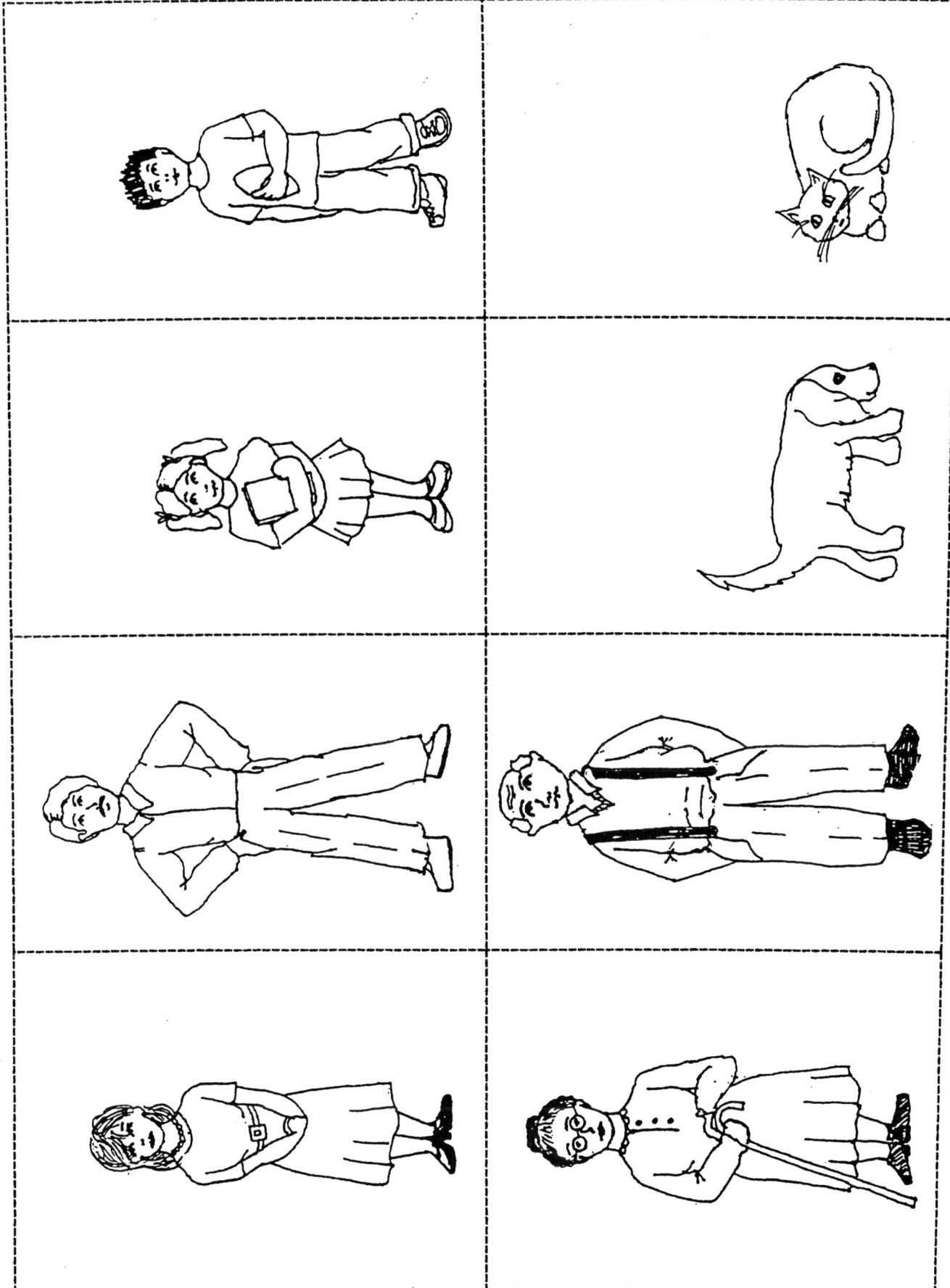

2e

2. Mi libro perdido
See page 2b for game and activity ideas using these vocabulary cards.

2. Mi libro perdido

See page 2b for game and activity ideas using these vocabulary cards.

2g

3. Las siete iguanas

Words and music by Patti Lozano

Arriba en las montañas   vivían siete iguanas
Y todas muy sanas - ¡pero miren que pasó!

1. La iguana más grande   se enfermó bastante
   Y ahora en las montañas, hay sólo seis iguanas

2. La iguana mediana   se fue para Indiana
   Y ahora en las montañas, hay sólo cinco iguanas

3. La iguana más pequeña   fue en busca de su cena
   Y ahora en las montañas, hay sólo cuatro iguanas

4. La iguana más gorda   se quedó sorda
   Y ahora en las montañas, hay sólo tres iguanas

5. La iguana más delgada   la hicieron ensalada
   Y ahora en las montañas, hay sólo dos iguanas

6. La iguana más bonita   le mató la abuelita
   Y ahora en las montañas,   hay sólo una iguana

7. La iguana más fea   subió la chimenea
   Y ahora en las montañas   ya no hay iguanas

Arriba en las montañas   vivían siete iguanas
Pero iguanas muy sanas en las montañas -
¡Ya no hay!

Up in the mountains lived 7 iguanas
And all very healthy - but look what happened!

The biggest iguana became very ill
And now in the mountains, there's only 6 iguanas

The middle-sized iguana went to Indiana
And now... there's only 5 iguanas

The smallest iguana went looking for his dinner
And now... there's only 4 iguanas

The fattest iguana became deaf
And now... there's only 3 iguanas

The skinniest iguana was made into salad
And now... there's only 2 iguanas

The prettiest iguana was killed by the grandmother
And now... there's only 1 iguana

The ugliest iguana climbed the chimney
And now... there are no iguanas

High up in the mountains lived seven iguanas
But very healthy iguanas in the mountains
There are none!

3. Las siete iguanas
Teaching Suggestions

Language Objectives: Descriptive Adjectives, Superlatives

☺ Vocabulary (in order of appearance in the song):

Adjectives:	Superlatives
grande *(big)*	**la ..... más grande** *(the biggest.....)*
mediano(a) *(medium)*	
pequeño(a) *(little)*	**la ..... más pequeña** *(the littlest .....)*
gordo(a) *(fat)*	**la ..... más gorda** *(the fattest .....)*
delgado(a) *(thin)*	**la ..... más delgada** *(the thinnest.....)*
bonito(a) *(pretty)*	**la ..... más bonita** *(the prettiest .....)*
feo(a) *(ugly)*	**la ..... más fea** *(the ugliest .....)*

☺ Structures:

Comparatives - when *más* precedes the adjective, it becomes a comparative.
  For example: *Esta mesa es más fea.* (This table is uglier.)
          Este perro es más pequeño que ese. (This dog is littler than that one.)
Superlatives - When *el más/la más/los más/las más* precedes the adjective, it becomes a superlative. For example:
  Esta mesa es la más fea. (This is the ugliest table.)
  Este perro es el más pequeño. (This is the littlest dog.)

☺ Cultural Note: The iguana is a tropical lizard. It has a crest of spiny scales down its back and may be big or small. In Mexico, Central and South American countries children sometimes keep them as pets. They may grow to be sixteen feet long!

☺ Extension Vocabulary:
  More adjectives and opposites

suave/duro(a) *(soft/hard)*	**feroz/tímido(a)** *(fierce/timid)*
limpio(a)/sucio(a) *(clean/dirty)*	**joven/viejo(a)** *(young/old)*
triste/feliz *(sad/happy)*	**alto(a)/bajo(a)** *(tall/short)*
largo(a)/corto(a) *(long/short)*	**inteligente/estúpido(a)** *(intelligent/stupid)*
cómico(a)/serio(a) *(funny/serious)*	**bueno(a)/malo(a)** *(good/bad)*

Extension Games and Activities:

A. **Parade of Iguanas**
  Spread a long sheet of white butcher paper on the floor or tape it to the wall. Each student draws and colors an iguana, then writes a sentence about it below the creation. The sentence might say, *"La iguana es roja y verde, y es delgada."* Have each student share his iguana and read his description. The teacher might then ask questions, for example;
  ¿Cuál iguana es la más bonita?
  ¿Cuál iguana es la más gorda?
  ¿Cuál iguana es la más larga?

B. **Seeing Stars**
Cut lots of photos of celebrities and movie scenes out of magazines such as People™ and Entertainment Weekly™. Paste each photo to index stock paper. (These "flashcards" may be used for many different exercises throughout the year.) Pair students and give each pair about 10 flashcards that they must spread out face down between them. Instruct them not to look at the photos prior to the activity. Student A says three adjectives and then turns over a card. He gets a point for every adjective that describes that celebrity or scene. Now it is Student B's turn to name three adjectives and turn over another card. The activity continues until all cards are turned over, and the student with the highest number of points wins.

C. **Adjective Art**
Distribute a copy of page 3d to each student. Spend a bit of time introducing and practicing the names of common shapes:

| el cuadrado | el círculo | el rectángulo | el diamante | el triángulo | la estrella |

Play an atmospheric CD without lyrics (perhaps some Andean folk songs) and let the students draw something in each shape on the page according to the instructions, also on page 3d, involving adjectives.
When the students are finished, they may share their favorite two drawings with the class, describing them such as;
  *"Hay un bebé en el círculo porque un bebé es bonito y pequeño.
  Santa Claus está el el cuadrado porque Santa Claus es grande y gordo..."*

Make it Meaningful

Mi familia
Ask students to bring photos of family and/or friends and to describe each person present in the photo. For example:
  "Este es el cumpleaños de mi hermano, David. Mi hermano es pequeño y bajo. Tiene cinco años. Esta es mi tía Maria. María es bonita y delgada y su vestido es azul...."

The Song as a Teaching Tool

Who said that only seven iguanas lived on those mountains?! Let's put twelve iguanas there, and make up some new verses for the additional five! Kids can make up verses. They don't really have to rhyme and they may be in the present tense... or you may try the following ones:

La iguana más larga... se puso amarga... (The longest iguana... became bitter...)
La iguana más suave... se puso miserable... (The softest iguana... became miserable...)
La iguana más feliz... se fue a Hollywood para ser actriz... (The happiest iguana... went to
  Hollywood to be an actress...)
La iguana más corta... se escondió en una torta... (The shortest iguana... hid in a cake...)
La iguana más dura... se lastimó la cintura... (The hardest iguana... hurt his waist...)

3. Las siete iguanas

Arriba en las montañas vivían siete iguanas,
Y todas muy sanas - ¡pero mira que pasó!

1. La iguana más grande se enfermó bastante
   Y ahora en las montañas, hay sólo seis iguanas

2. La iguana mediana se fue para Indiana
   Y ahora en las montañas, hay sólo cinco iguanas

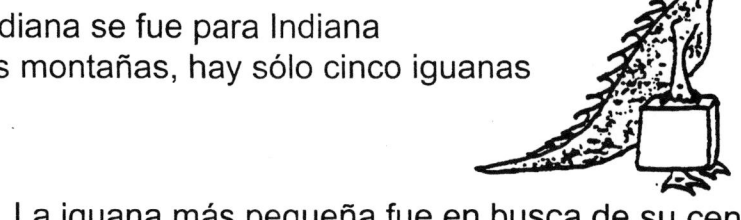

3. La iguana más pequeña fue en busca de su cena
   Y ahora en las montañas, hay sólo cuatro iguanas

4. La iguana más gorda se quedó sorda
   Y ahora en las montañas, hay sólo tres iguanas

5. La iguana más delgada la hicieron ensalada
   Y ahora en las montañas, hay sólo dos iguanas

6. La iguana más bonita le mató la abuelita
   Y ahora en las montañas, hay sólo una iguana

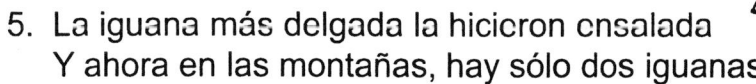

7. La iguana más fea subió la chimenea
   Y ahora en las montañas, ¡ya no hay iguanas!

Arriba en las montañas vivían siete iguanas
Pero iguanas muy sanas en las montañas -
¡Ya no hay!

3. Las siete iguanas

Dibuja algo pequeño y bonito en el círculo.
Dibuja algo feo y sucio en el triángulo.
Dibuja algo limpio y nuevo en el rectángulo.
Dibuja algo grande y gordo en el cuadrado.
Dibuja algo delgado y viejo en la estrella.
[Bonus] Dibuja algo bajo y suave en el diamante.
[Bonus] En otro papel, dibuja la forma que tú quieres.
     Dibuja algo adentro y descríbelo.

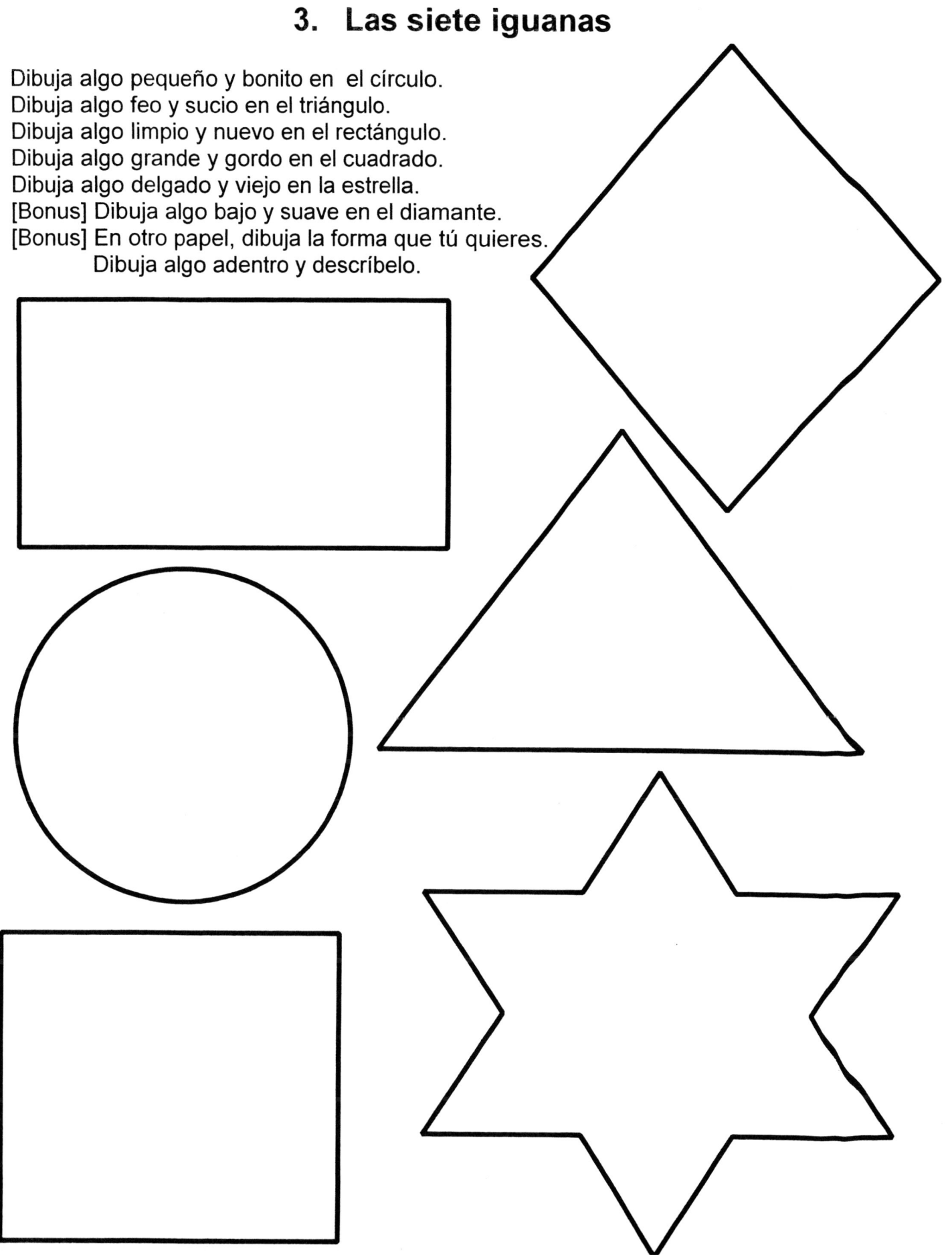

4. El rancho de Pancho

Words and music by Patti Lozano

Estribillo:
  El rancho de Pancho es bonito
  El rancho de Pancho es especial
  Porque Pancho no quiere uno -
  Pancho siempre quiere dos de cada animal
  Pancho quiere dos de cada animal
  Y Pancho dice -

Refrain:
  Pancho's farm is pretty
  Pancho's farm is special
  Because Pancho doesn't want one -
  Pancho always wants two of every animal
  Pancho wants two of every animal
  And Pancho says -

Versos:
1. "Un caballo nunca - no, no, no, no, nunca
   Un caballo nunca contento está
   Dos caballos siempre - sí, sí, sí, sí, siempre,
   Dos caballos siempre contentos están"

Verses:
1. *"One horse never - no, no, no, no, never*
   One horse is never happy
   Two horses always - yes, yes, yes, yes, always
   Two horses are always happy"

2. "Una vaca nunca - no, no, no, no, nunca
   Una vaca nunca contenta está
   Dos vacas siempre - sí, sí, sí, sí, siempre,
   Dos vacas siempre contentas están"

2. *"One cow never - no, no, no, no, never*
   One cow is never happy
   Two cows always - yes, yes, yes, yes, always
   Two cows are always happy"

3. "Una oveja nunca ...

3. *One sheep never...*

4. El rancho de Pancho
Teaching Suggestions

Language Objectives: Farm and Domestic Animals
☺ Vocabulary:
- **el rancho** *(farm, ranch)*
- **la vaca** *(cow)*
- **nunca** *(never)*
- **contento(a)** *(happy)*
- **el caballo** *(horse)*
- **la oveja** *(sheep)*
- **siempre** *(always)*

☺ Grammar Notes:
The definite articles are *"el"* and *"la"* (singular) and *"los"* and *"las"* (plural). This is the equivalent of the English word, "the".
The indefinite articles are *"un"* and *"una"* (singular) and *"unos"* and *"unas"* (plural). These are the equivalents of the English words, "a" and "an" (singular) and "some" (plural).
To make a plural noun in Spanish just add an "s".
(Example: *"el caballo... los caballos"*   *"una vaca... unas vacas"*)

☺ *Extension Vocabulary: (more farm and domestic animals)
- **el cerdo** *(pig)*
- **el pato** *(duck)*
- **el perro** *(dog)*
- **el perico** *(parrot)*
- **la llama** *(llama)*
- **la gallina** *(hen)*
- **el gato** *(cat)*
- **el ratoncito** *(mouse)*
- **el pez/los peces** *(fish)*

* All animals are illustrated on flashcards on page 4d.

Extension Games and Activities:

A. **Butcher Paper Farm**
Pancho is about to have a very big ranch! Display a long piece of white butcher paper and have colored pens available for students. Student B gives Student A instructions as to which animal and how many to draw (up to 5 of the same animal.) Student B may name any animal he knows from the target vocabulary and extension vocabulary lists and pictures. Continue with Student C telling Student B what to draw. After each student has drawn, the class recites the numbers and kinds of animals Pancho now has on his farm. Example:
Student B to Student A; *Pancho tiene 3 patos en el rancho.* [Student A draws them.]
Class: *El rancho de Pancho tiene 3 patos.*
Student C to Student B: *Pancho tiene 2 perros en el rancho.* [Student B draws them.]
Class: *El rancho de Pancho tiene 3 patos y 2 perros.*
Student D to Student C: *Pancho tiene 1 pato y 4 peces en el rancho.* [Student C draws them.]
Class: *El rancho de Pancho tiene 4 patos, 2 perros y 4 peces.*
As you can see, the class must continually add the new animals to the old drawings. The students seated may have pencil and paper to help keep a record of the number of each animal drawn.

B. **Hay cuatro caballos...** Copy as many pages of flashcard page 4d as you have students and cut them into individual cards. Place all of the cards in a paper bag and shake the bag well to mix them up. Have each student grab a handful (about twelve cards.) Each student will have a different assortment of animal cards. Students sort their cards and then take turns saying what animals they each have on their farm. For example:

"En mi rancho hay seis cerdos, dos peces, tres caballos y una gallina."

If any two or more students have exactly the same mix, they receive a prize (like a goldfish cracker!)

C. The game board template on page 4e must be prepared by the teacher in order to play **"Ranchero compañero"**. Make a class set of these boards, putting different numbers in the blanks and different colors in the circles. Each board must have exactly ONE identical matching board. For example, one board might say:

This would mean that the holder of this card has *"cuatro vacas negras"* and *"dos patos blancos"*. The object of the activity is for each *"ranchero"* in your class to find his one *"compañero,"* i.e. the person with the matching card. They must find their partners without looking at each other's cards. Students mill around the room, peeking at their own cards and asking others questions like, *"¿Cuántos gatos hay en tu rancho?"* If they discover that they have the same number of cats, they now ask about the cats' color or about another animal. They must go through most of the card to ascertain that they are indeed *compañeros*.

Make it Meaningful

Ask students to think about the pets they know on their street or in their apartment complex. Have them tell the class about three of the most interesting pets. They should use the adjectives learned in Song #3, *"Las siete iguanas"* in their descriptions!   Here's an example:

"En mi colonia hay un perro que se llama Roger. Roger es blanco y negro, y es mediano. Penny es un perro muy inteligente y feliz, pero es muy feroz con los gatos..."

The Song as a Teaching Tool

Some animal sounds are different in Spanish, for example:
El perro dice – ¡Guau guau!   *El caballo dice – ¡Ji ji jiii!*
La vaca dice – ¡Mu!   *El gato dice – ¡Miau!*
La gallina dice – ¡Clo clo clo! *El pato dice – ¡Cuac cuac!*

Sing the song... add as many additional verses as you want, and in each verse, instead of singing the animal name, make the animal sound, like this:

"Un ji ji jiii nunca, no, no, no, no, nunca,   Un ji ji jiii nunca contento está..."

Note: *Las ovejas* still say, *"¡Baaa baaa!"* *Los peces* say nothing, but kids can make fishy faces!

4. El rancho de Pancho

Estribillo:
El rancho de Pancho es bonito
El rancho de Pancho es especial
Porque Pancho no quiere uno -
Pancho siempre quiere dos de cada animal
Pancho quiere dos de cada animal
Y Pancho dice -

1. "Un caballo nunca, no, no, no, no, nunca
   Un caballo nunca contento está.
   Dos caballos siempre, sí, sí, sí. sí, siempre,
   Dos caballos siempre contentos están."

2. "Una vaca nunca, no, no, no, no, nunca
   Una vaca nunca contenta está.
   Dos vacas siempre, sí, sí, sí, sí, siempre,
   Dos vacas siempre contentas están."

3. "Una oveja nunca, no, no, no, no, nunca
   Una oveja nunca contenta está.
   Dos ovejas siempre, sí, sí, sí, sí, siempre,
   Dos ovejas siempre contentas están."

4. El rancho de Pancho

See page 4b for game and activity ideas using these vocabulary cards.

4. El rancho de Pancho

See page 4b for instructions on how to do this group activity.

5. Soy un pajarito

Words and music by Patti Lozano

Soy un pajarito, ¡mira qué bonito!
Mírame volar en el cielo azul
Soy un pajarito, ¡mira qué bonito!
Mírame volar en el cielo azul
1. Arriba (echo) abajo (echo)
    Arriba (echo) abajo (echo)
Así estoy contento
Pero no quiero estar adentro (echo)
Adentro (echo)
Adentro de la jaula

2. Cerca de / lejos de
3. Sobre / debajo de
4. Delante de / detrás de

I'm a little bird, Look how pretty!
Look at me fly in the blue sky
I'm a little bird, Look how pretty!
Look at me fly in the blue sky
1. Up (echo) down (echo)
    Up (echo) down (echo)
This way I am happy
But I don't want to be inside (echo)
Inside (echo)
Inside of the cage

2. Near / far from
3. On top of / under
4. In front of / behind

5. Soy un pajarito
Teaching Suggestions

Language Objectives: Prepositions
- ☺ Vocabulary: **arriba** *(up)*   **abajo** *(down)*
  cerca (de) *(near)*   **lejos (de)** *(far)*
  sobre *(on top of)*   **debajo (de)** *(under)*
  delante (de) *(in front of)*   **detrás (de)** *(behind)*
  adentro (de) *(inside)*   **el pajarito** *(little bird)*
  el cielo *(sky)*   **la jaula** *(cage)*

- ☺ Structures: There are no targeted structures in this unit.

- ☺ Extension Vocabulary: (More prepositions)
  entre *(between)*   **alrededor** *(around, round)*
  al lado (de) *(by the side of)*   **hacia** *(toward, towards)*

Extension Games and Activities:

A. **Pájaro y jaula** *(Bird and cage)*
Distribute a copy of page 5d (the bird) to each student. Allow students to color in their birds, but you assign the color that each bird's head is to be, making sure that every color is represented. (You may want to laminate the birds at this point, so you can use them in subsequent years.) Also, attach a wooden popsicle stick to the stomach of each bird, so students may hold it as they would a paper fan. Pick half of the students to be the *"birds"*; then each bird picks a classmate to be her *"cage"*. Line the students up along the front of the room in *bird - cage, bird - cage*, order. "Cages" have their arms in a circle in front of their bodies, fingers tightly interlocked to be the unyielding steel bars of the cage. As the CD is played, the students holding birds role play the choreography in the song (flying up, flying down, etc.) using the "cage" as a reference point. When the lyrics say, *"No quiero estar adentro... adentro... adentro de la jaula..."* the bird flies into the cage and beats it's body against the bars to escape, but of course, it can't.

B. **El vuelo de los pájaros** *(The Flight of the Birds)*
Have eleven students in front of the room. Each holds a bird with a different color head. Make a set of flashcards of the 9 - 13 prepositions on index stock. Hold the flashcards fanned out like a deck of cards, with the words facing you. Walk around and let students that do not have birds take turns to choose a flashcard, read the word and then make a statement directed to one or more of the colored-headed birds in the front of the room.
For example:
Student A chooses the flashcard *"cerca de"* and makes up a sentence: *"El pájaro azul está cerca del pájaro morado."* The two birds named, in this case the blue-headed bird and the purple-headed bird, move close to each other.
Now Student B happens to pick the flashcard *"entre"*. He makes up this sentence: *"El pájaro amarillo está entre el pájaro negro y el pájaro blanco."* The black-headed bird and the white-headed bird move to stand at each side of the yellow-headed bird.
★Variation: You may use the same activity to review classroom objects.

C. Build it!

Bring a big bag of Legos™ or small colored wooden or plastic blocks to class. Divide students into groups of 3-4 and give each group a pile of blocks. The teams build structures according to the teacher's instructions. For example:

> "Toma el cuadrado rojo. Pon un rectángulo blanco sobre el cuadrado rojo. Pon un cuadrado verde y largo debajo del cuadrado rojo... etc."

★Variation: One team builds a structure as they instruct the other teams to build a similar structure by following their instructions.

Make it Meaningful

A Friend-ly Arrangement

On his/her own, each student quietly chooses 5 - 7 classmates and then explains on paper how he plans to group and arrange them in front of the room. He writes a sentence that places each student on his list. Give each student a turn to describe his or her arrangement. For example:

> "Mario está detrás de Linda. Maribel está al lado de Linda. David está lejos del grupo. Felix está debajo de la mano de Maribel. Clara está cerca de Felix. El zapato de Clara está sobre el zapato de Felix... etc."

As the arrangement is described, each selected student takes his place in the tableau at the front of the room. Take a photo of each arrangement, attach it to the arranger's paper, and display them all on a bulletin board. Fun, interactive, meaningful and creative!

The Song as a Teaching Tool

This is one of the few times in this book that a song activity is geared toward someone with a bit of musical training! You may reinforce the prepositions by creating a beautiful harmony sung on a descending scale during the singing of the refrain. The harmony is simply the familiar "Do, Re, Mi, Fa, Sol, La, Ti, Do" that everyone knows from the classic musical *"The Sound of Music"*), but sung in reverse, from high Do back down to low Do. Have half the class sing the chorus while the other half sings the harmony. Provide a gesture for each preposition. Here is the harmony with suggested gestures:

High Do – *arriba* – [hands in the air]
Ti – *abajo* – [hands towards floor]
La – *adentro de* – [hug self closely with arms]
Sol – *afuera de* – [arms out from each side]
Fa – *lejos de* – [lean way out with one arm]
Mi – *cerca de* – [fist against heart]
Re – *alredede...* – [palms out, and with large gestures...
Do – *... dor* – [make very large heart shape in front of torso]

By the way, on another musical note, did you realize that the melody of the chorus uses the same chord structure as Pachabel's beloved Canon? Any harmony that can be sung with Pachabel's Canon will also work with the chorus of **"Soy un pajarito"**.

5. Soy un pajarito

1. Arriba / abajo
2. Cerca de / lejos de
3. Sobre / debajo de
4. Delante de / detrás de

Soy un pajarito. ¡Mira qué bonito!
Mírame volar en el cielo azul
Soy un pajarito. ¡Mira qué bonito!
Mírame volar en el cielo azul.

1. Arriba (echo)   Abajo (echo)
   Arriba (echo)   Abajo (echo)

Así estoy contento
Pero no quiero estar adentro (echo)
Adentro (echo)
Adentro de la jaula

5. Soy un pajarito

See page 5b for game and activity instructions using this template.

5d

6. Derecha, izquierda y alrededor

Words and music by Patti Lozano

Primera parte:
Derecha, izquierda   derecha, izquierda
Derecha, izquierda   y alrededor
Derecha, izquierda   derecha, izquierda
Derecha, izquierda   y alrededor

Segunda parte:
Pasos adelante
Toca la tierra, toca el sol
Pasos atrás, y ¡olé!
Toca la tierra, toca el sol

Tercera parte:
Cruza con la pierna derecha y ¡zas!
Cruza con la pierna izquierda y ¡zas!
Cruza con la pierna derecha y ¡zas!
Cruza con la pierna izquierda y ¡zas!

First part:
Right, left   right, left
Right, left   and around
Right, left   right, left
Right, left   and around

Second part:
Steps forward
Touch the earth, touch the sun
Steps backward, and "Olé!"
Touch the earth, touch the sun

Third part:
Cross with the right leg and "zas!"
Cross with the left leg and "zas!"
Cross with the right leg and "zas!"
Cross with the left leg and "zas!"

6. Derecha, izquierda y alrededor
Teaching Suggestions

Language Objectives: Directions, Review of Prepositions
- Vocabulary: **derecha** *(the right [side])* **izquierda** *(the left [side])*
  a la derecha *(to the right)* **a la izquierda** *(to the left)*
  alrededor *(around)*
  pasos adelante *(forward steps)* **pasos atrás** *(backward steps)*
  toca la tierra *(touch the ground/earth)* **toca el sol** *(touch the sun)*
  cruza con la pierna derecha *(cross with the right foot)*
  cruza con la pierna izquierda *(cross with the left foot)*
  ¡Zas! *(An exclamatory sound)*

- Structures: There are no targeted structures in this unit.

Extension Games and Activities:

A. Page 6d is a depiction on a farm. In fact, it is Pancho's farm (from Song #4, *"El rancho de Pancho"*)! Have students fill the farm by drawing in animals according to the instructions on Page 6e. This creative activity combines and reviews the objectives from Songs #4, #5 and #6 (domestic animals, prepositions and directions).
Remind students that memorable works of art are not expected. Stick figure animals are fine. Also note that some animals will be drawn inside the enclosures on the farm, while others will roam free.

Make it Meaningful

Still Life
Ask each student to create a "Still Life" arrangement on a table at home using 4 - 8 common objects, and then to take a digital photo of it and to bring the photo to school. They must only arrange objects for which they know the Spanish words! Here's an example of a photo (on somewhat of an advanced level): ➡ The teacher looks at the photos and chooses one student to come to the front of the room. The student describes the photo, especially the colors and placement of all objects on the table, as the class tries to draw the scene according to the description – without actually seeing the photo. When the drawings are completed, compare them with the photo to see whose came the closest to replicating the photo.

The Song as a Teaching Tool

Choreography

This song may be sung in unison, or, once students know it well, as a three part-round. On the CD, it is first heard in unison. The following track has it performed as a round. The song may also be performed as a dance, meant to reinforce left and right, which may also be executed in unison, or, only once the students know the song very well— as a three-part dance. Here are the steps:

Part 1. *[Lyrics: "Derecha, izquierda, derecha, izquierda,*
derecha, izquierda, y alrededor"]
    Beats 1 - 8: Clap right, clap left, clap right, clap left, clap right, clap left, then on beats 7 & 8 turn around one complete time in four steps
    Beats 9 - 16: Repeat lyrics and movements from Beats 1 - 8

Part 2: *[Lyrics: "Pasos adelante   Toca la tierra, toca el sol"*
Pasos atrás y ¡olé!   Toca la tierra, toca el sol"]
    Beats 1 - 4: ("Pasos adelante") 4 steps forward, starting on the right foot, snap fingers after each step
    Beats 5 - 8: (beat 5) extend R hand down toward the ground, (beat 6) extend L hand down toward the ground; (beat 7) extend R hand up toward the sky, (beat 8) extend L hand up toward the sky
    Beats 9 - 12: ("Pasos atrás y ¡olé!) 4 steps and snaps backwards, and
    Beats 13 - 16: touch the ground and sky again

Part 3: [Lyrics: *"Cruza con la pierna derecha y ¡zas!*
Cruza con la pierna izquierda y ¡zas!"]
    Beats 1 - 8: Do a "grapevine" step, (moving to the left,) beginning with the R foot, crossing behind the L. Do six "grapevine" steps (6 beats), stand still on beat 7, and clap on beat 8.
    Beats 9 - 16: Do the reverse, moving back toward the right. This time the L foot begins, crossing in front of the R foot.

6. Derecha, izquierda y alrededor

La primera parte:
Derecha, izquierda, derecha, izquierda,
Derecha, izquierda y alrededor
Derecha, izquierda, derecha, izquierda,
Derecha, izquierda y alrededor

La segunda parte:
Pasos adelante
Toca la tierra, toca el sol
Pasos atrás y ¡olé!
Toca la tierra, toca el sol

La tercera parte:
Cruza con la pierna derecha y ¡zas!
Cruza con la pierna izquierda y ¡zas!
Cruza con la pierna derecha y ¡zas!
Cruza con la pierna izquierda y ¡zas!

6. Derecha, izquierda y alrededor

See page 6b for activity instructions. See the back of this page for drawing directions.

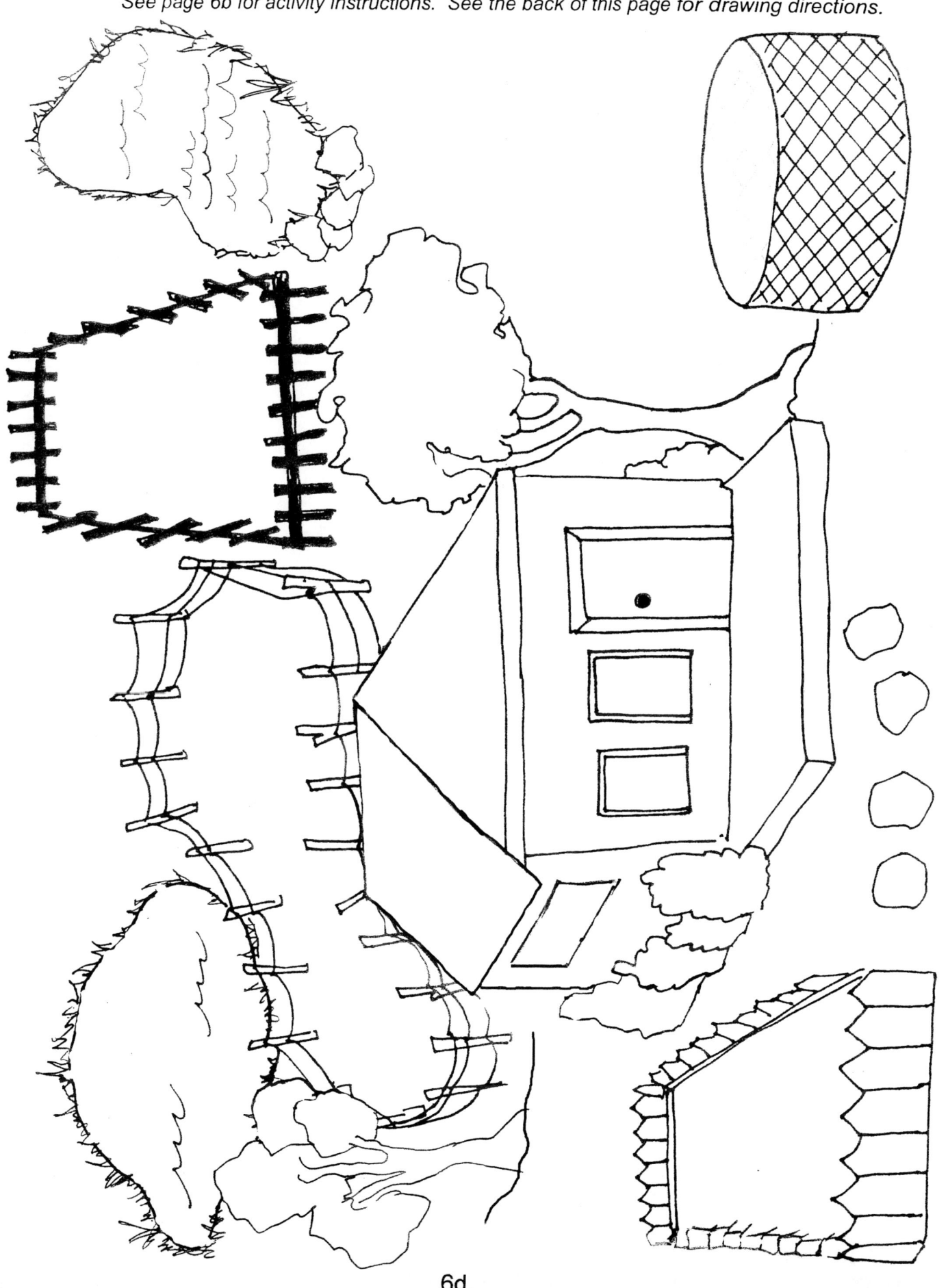

6d

6. Derecha, izquierda y alrededor

¡Bienvenido al rancho de Pancho! ¿Pero dónde están los animales?

You draw the animal to fill Pancho's farm by following the instructions below.

- Pancho tiene dos gatos. Los gatos están adentro de la casa. Los gatos miran por las ventanas.

- Pancho tiene dos patos. Los patos nadan en el lago a la izquierda detrás de la casa.

- Pancho tiene dos caballos. Los caballos están delante del lago de patos, detrás de la casa.

- Pancho tiene cinco gallinas. Las gallinas están delante de la casa.

- Pancho tiene dos cerdos. Los cerdos están a la izquierda de la casa.

- Pancho tiene muchos peces. Los peces están debajo del agua en el lago a la derecha, detrás de la casa.

- Pancho tiene dos ovejas. Las ovejas están entre los caballos y el lago de peces.

- Pancho tiene dos perros. Un perro está delante de la casa. El otro perro está en el rancho también, pero está muy lejos de la casa.

- Pancho tiene dos vacas. Una vaca toma el agua del lago a la derecha. La otra vaca toma el agua del lago a la izquierda.

- Pancho tiene dos llamas. Están a la izquierda de la casa cerca del árbol grande. Una llama está adentro del corral, y la otra llama está cerca, pero está afuera del corral.

- No hay ratoncitos en el rancho de Pancho.

- Pancho no tiene pericos, pero hay dos pájaros arriba en el árbol grande.

7. Quiero viajar en un coche azul

Words and music by Patti Lozano

[Sheet music]

Quiero viajar en un coche azul
Quiero ver el mundo en un coche azul
Ahora soy joven, pero cuando sea grande
Quiero viajar en un coche azul

No importa si es nuevo,
No importa si es viejo,
No importa si es limpio o sucio,
No importa si va lento o va rápido,
Lo importante es que sea azul
Lo importante es que sea azul

2. un autobús azul
3. un avión azul
4. un barco azul

I want to travel in a blue car
I want to see the world in a blue car
Now I'm young, but when I'm old
I want to travel in a blue car

It doesn't matter if it's new,
It doesn't matter if it's old
It doesn't matter if it's clean or dirty
It doesn't matter if it's slow or fast
The important thing is that it be blue
The important thing is that it be blue

2. a blue bus
3. a blue airplane
4. a blue boat

7. Quiero viajar en un coche azul
Teaching Suggestions

Language Objectives: Transportation, Adjectives
- ☺ Vocabulary: **el coche** *(car)*   **el autobús** *(bus)*
  el avión *(airplane)*   **el barco** *(boat)*
  nuevo(a) *(new)*   **viejo(a)** *(old)*
  limpio(a) *(clean)*   **sucio(a)** *(clean)*
  lento *(slowly)*   **rápido** *(fast)*

- ☺ Structures: **Quiero viajar...** *(I want to travel...)*
  Quiero ver el mundo... *(I want to see the world...)*
  No importa si es... *(I don't care if it's...)*

- ☺ Extension Vocabulary: (corresponds to the transportation illustrations on pages 7d)
  la bicicleta *(bicycle)*   **el elefante** *(elephant)*
  el caballo *(horse)*   **el globo** *(hot air balloon)*
  el camión *(truck)*   **la motocicleta** *(motorcycle)*
  el tren *(train)*   **de pie** *(on foot)*

  Additional Vocabulary (for activities, not illustrated)
  el camello *(camel)*   **la camioneta** *(minivan)*

Extension Games and Activities:

A. **Pepe no puede pasar** *(Pepe can't pass by)*
Teach this short rhyme to the class in preparation for the active transportation game that follows:
*"Pepe no puede pasar. Pepe quiere gritar.
Pepe no puede pasar al palacio, Pepe no puede pasar."*

Pepe no puede pasar — Game Directions
1. Distribute a transportation vocabulary card (page 7d) to each student in class. You may also use photos of modes of transportation cut from magazines.
2. Arrange the class in a circle.
3. As everyone chants the first two lines, walk around the circle pointing to students, one student per beat. The eighth student (8th beat) becomes "it" and goes to the circle center with his vocabulary card and states, *"Pepe no puede pasar al parque porque hay un _____ [vocabulary card word here] en el camino."* He stays in the center as the class repeats his sentence, and then all say the last line of the chant.
4. Continue the activity from Step 3 again, starting with pointing to the next child in the circle. This second child names two reasons that Pepe can't pass by, saying *"Pepe no puede pasar al parque porque hay un _____ y un _____ en el camino."* Continue with this cumulative activity as more and more students stand in the center of the circle, and the sentences get longer and longer.
   ★Variations: Each student adds an adjective after he names his vocabulary card.
   Each student devises a gesture to go with his vocabulary card.

B. **Utilize the vocabulary cards**
   Distribute a copy of page 7d to each student. Color the transportation objects. Students then write a complete sentence in each box, pertaining to the illustration. For example:
   Quiero viajar a Arkansas en un coche nuevo.
   No quiero viajar a Hawaii de pie.

C. **Clever Comparisons**
   Make a transparency of page 7d and cut out the squares so you have a deck of 12 cards. Cover each card with a Post It Note.™ Shuffle the pictures and place them all on the overhead projector. Choose a student to come up and pull the Post It Note off two cards. The student must identify the two modes of transportation, and must quickly list one way in which they are both similar, and any other way in which they are different. For example:
   Student uncovers: *elefante* and *autobús*
   El mismo (Same): *El elefante y el autobús son grandes.*
   Diferente (Different): *El elefante tiene orejas y el autobús tiene sillas.*

Make it Meaningful

Have two students stand next to a globe and give it a spin. With their eyes closed, students point to locations on the globe when it stops spinning. They open their eyes and place a dot or sticky arrow on the chosen place. Students must name the countries, and then decide the best way to travel from one country to the other.
★Variation: One student chooses a country (eyes closed), and must list appropriate means of travel within that country. This is an excellent way to review topography.
★Variation: Use this activity to review weather also!

The Song as a Teaching Tool

The Wonderful Change-a-Word Chant
   Make a transparency graph that contains one phrase from the song, as per the example on page 7e. Follow these instructions for a delightful activity that combines structure, syntax and creativity!
1. The entire class chants the line twice.
2. Any student raises his hand and shouts out a replacement for any one word. For example, the student shouts out, *"visitar"* which obviously replaces the word, *"ver"*. Write the replacement word in the box under the original word.
3. All students now chant the new sentence twice, which in this case is, *"Quiero visitar el mundo en un coche azul."*
4. Continue changing the words one-word-at-a-time until the class is chanting an entirely new, and often odd or humorous, sentence. Only then do you begin to change the lyrics on the second row of the graph.
Note: Sometimes prepositions may need to be added, articles and endings might change – this is the beauty of the Change-a-Word Chant!

7. Quiero viajar en un coche azul

Quiero viajar en un coche azul
Quiero ver el mundo en un coche azul
Ahora soy joven, pero cuando sea grande
Quiero viajar en un coche azul

No importa si es nuevo, no importa si es viejo

No importa si es limpio o sucio,

No importa si va lento o va rápido,

Lo importante es que sea azul,
¡Lo importante es que sea azul!

2. Quiero viajar en un autobús azul
   Quiero ver el mundo en un autobús azul
   Ahora soy joven, pero cuando sea grande
   Quiero viajar en un autobús azul

3. Quiero viajar en un avión azul
   Quiero ver el mundo en un avión azul
   Ahora soy joven, pero cuando sea grande
   Quiero viajar en un avión azul

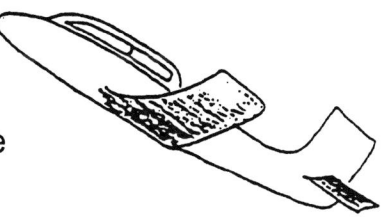

4. Quiero viajar en un barco azul
   Quiero ver el mundo en un barco azul
   Ahora soy joven, pero cuando sea grande
   Quiero viajar en un barco azul

7. Quiero viajar en un coche azul

See page 7b for game and activity ideas using these vocabulary cards.

7. Quiero viajar en un coche azul

See page 7b for instructions on how to use this template.

azul.					
un coche					
en					
el mundo					
ver					
Quiero					

8. Cáscara de coco, jugo de piña

Words and music by Patti Lozano

Estribillo:
    Cáscara de coco, jugo de piña
    Un popote con parasol   (2X)

1. Una ballena salta alto
   Y tomo el sol en la playa tropical (2X)

2. Dos delfines juegan juntos
   Y tomo el sol en la playa tropical (2X)

3. Tres tiburones buscan peces
   Y tomo el sol en la playa tropical (2X)

4. Cuatro conchas flotan a la arena
   Y tomo el sol en la playa tropical (2X)

5. Cinco pulpos se esconden
   Y tomo el sol en la playa tropical (2X)

Refrain:
    Coconut shell, pineapple juice
    A straw with a parasol   (2X)

1. *One whale jumps up high*
   And I sunbathe on the tropical beach (2X)

2. *Two dolphins play together*
   And I sunbathe on the tropical beach (2X)

3. *Three sharks search for fish*
   And I sunbathe on the tropical beach (2X)

4. *Four shells float to the sand*
   And I sunbathe on the tropical beach (2X)

5. *Five octopuses hide themselves*
   And I sunbathe on the tropical beach (2X)

8. Cáscara de coco, jugo de piña
Teaching Suggestions

Language Objectives: Sea Animals
- ☺ Vocabulary:

Sea animal	*Action*
la ballena (whale)	**salta alto** (jumps up high)
los delfines (dolphins)	**juegan juntos** (play together)
los tiburones (sharks)	**buscan peces** (look for fish)
las conchas (seashells)	**flotan a la arena** (float to the sand)
los pulpos (octopus)	**se esconden** (hide)

el mar (the sea) [This word is not in the song, but is helpful for this unit!]
(la) cáscara de coco (coconut shell)
(el) jugo de piña (pineapple juice)
un popote con parasol (a straw with a [little paper] umbrella)

- ☺ Structures: The actions of each sea animal are listed above in Vocabulary section.

- ☺ Extension Vocabulary: (corresponds to the sea animal illustrations on pages 8d)

la ballena (whale)	**el tiburón** (shark)
la concha (seashell)	**el pez (plural: los peces)** (fish)
el coral (coral)	**la medusa** (jellyfish)
el camarón (shrimp)	**el delfín** (dolphin)
la estrella del mar (starfish)	**la tortuga** (turtle)
el pulpo (octopus)	**el cangrejo** (crab)

Extension Games and Activities:

A. Seascape
Unroll a long sheet of white or blue butcher paper to stretch across the floor. The butcher paper is the sea. Pair students. Student A takes off his shoes and lies on the floor, positioning himself so that his legs, at least from knee to foot, are on the butcher paper. Student B draws an outline of Student A's legs on the butcher paper. Now everyone in the class draws colorful sea animals from the song and extension vocabulary. They may be swimming in the ocean, resting on the sea floor in the sand, peeking into sunken ships – or even nipping at peoples' legs! Label the animals and the owner of the legs!

B. Go Fishing
Copy several sets of the sea animals on page 8d on index stock paper and cut them out. Attach a paper clip to each. Spread a blue sheet on the floor (that's the sea) and spread the sea animal cards face down all around. Create several fishing poles with a dowel rod, a string and a magnet attached to the end. Now the students may go fishing. Students must be able to name the sea animals they catch on their poles in order to keep them. If a student cannot name his animal he must unhook it and throw it back into the water.

C. **La lotería** *(The Lottery)*
Copy and distribute a complete set of the sea animal vocabulary cards (page 8d) to each student. Each student chooses cards and puts the rest away. The teacher also chooses three cards from his/her deck, and then calls out the chosen animals' names, for example, *"¡Tengo el coral... el tiburón... y el pulpo!"* All students that have the exact same three animal cards in their hands win the lottery (and receive a small favor).
(Students must prove that they have the winning cards by holding them up and saying the names of the sea creatures.)

D. **"To Say or Not to Say"**
Display the entire page 8d on a transparency or a doc cam. Point to any animal and make a statement. If your statement is correct or true, the students repeat it. If your statement is incorrect or false, the students stay completely silent. This works on many levels, for example:
1) To simply review vocabulary, i.e. point to *"el cangrejo"* and say *"el cangrejo"* or, incorrectly, say, *"el camarón"*
2) To reinforce grammar, i.e. point to *"el pez"* and say *"el pez"* or, incorrectly, *"la pez"*
3) To reinforce animal facts, i.e. *"Las ballenas comen animales muy pequeñas."* (This is correct.) Or... *"La ballena come la maestra."* This is both incorrect and funny.

Make it Meaningful

As a special project, invite students to make an Under-the-Sea diorama at home using a shoe box and pebbles, sand, grasses, and cut-outs of sea creatures, etc. Display each diorama and let each student talk about his own work.

The Song as a Teaching Tool

Have students change the lyrics to the refrain. Instead of singing, *"Cáscara de coco, jugo de piña, un popote con parasol,"* they create a refrain (same melody) from the names of the sea animals. Some words, because of syllables and natural accents, fit better than others. Here's an example of a refrain that sings quite nicely without distorting any words:

> *"Camarón y delfín, pulpo y ballena,*
> *Tiburón y la estrella del mar..."*

Students may hold up the appropriate sea animal cards as they sing their lyrics.

8. Cáscara de coco, jugo de piña

Estribillo:
Cáscara de coco, jugo de piña
Un popote con parasol (2X)

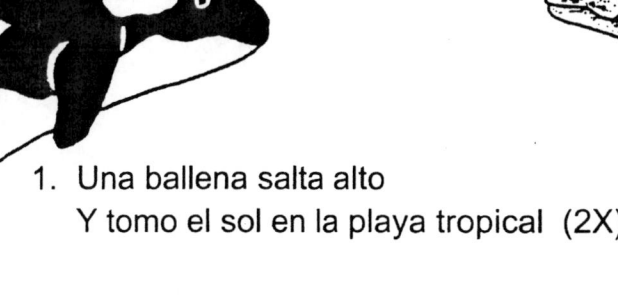

1. Una ballena salta alto
   Y tomo el sol en la playa tropical (2X)

2. Dos delfines juegan juntos
   Y tomo el sol en la playa tropical (2X)

3. Tres tiburones buscan peces
   Y tomo el sol en la playa tropical (2X)

4. Cuatro conchas flotan a la arena
   Y tomo el sol en la playa tropical

5. Cinco pulpos se esconden
   Y tomo el sol en la playa tropical (2X)

8. Cáscara de coco, jugo de piña

See page 8b for game and activity ideas using these vocabulary cards.

9. ¡Vamos a cantar! (Yo canto, tú cantas)

Words and music by Patti Lozano

1. ¡Vamos a cantar! (Yo canto, tú cantas) (2X)
   ¡Vamos a cantar! (Yo canto, tú cantas) (2X)
   La cabeza, la cintura, el corazón
   Pon las manos en cada rodilla
   ¡Vamos a cantar! (Yo canto, tú cantas)
   Hasta la hora de cenar

1. Let's sing! (I sing, you sing) (2X)
   Let's sing! (I sing, you sing) (2X)
   The head, the waist, the heart,
   Put your hands upon each knee
   Let's sing! (I sing, you sing)
   Until suppertime

Otros versos:

2. ¡Vamos a pintar! (Yo pinto, tú pintas)

3. ¡Vamos a nadar! (Yo nado, tú nadas)

4. ¡Vamos a leer! (Yo leo, tú lees)

5. ¡Vamos a jugar! (Yo juego, tú juegas)

Additional verses:

2. Let's paint! (I paint, you paint)

3. Let's swim! (I swim, you swim)

4. Let's read! (I read, you read)

5. Let's play! (I play, you play)

9. ¡Vamos a cantar! (Yo canto, tú cantas)
Teaching Suggestions

Language Objectives: Present Tense Regular Verb Forms (1st and 2nd person singular)

☺ Vocabulary: *Action verbs (as they appear in the song)*
    cantar *(to sing)*
    pintar *(to paint)*
    nadar *(to swim)*
    leer *(to read)*
    jugar *(to play a game or sport)*

    Body parts (review and new extension words)
    la cabeza *(head)*
    la cintura *(waist)*
    el corazón *(heart)*
    las manos *(hands)*
    la rodilla *(knee)*

☺ Structures: **Vamos a...** *(Let's....)*
<u>Conjugation of 1st pers. singular **"yo"** *(I)* and 2nd pers. singular **"tú"** *(you)*</u>
For *ar* verbs; take the *"ar"* off the infinitive, add *"o"* for *"yo"* and *"as"* for *"tú"*
Examples: infinitive: *cantar: Yo cant-o, tú cant-as*
          "   " *pintar: yo pint-o. tú pint-as*
For *er* verbs; take the *"er"* off the infinitive, add *"o"* for *"yo"* and *"es"* for *"tú"*
Examples: infinitive: *leer: Yo le-o, tú le-es*
For *ir* verbs; take the *"ir"* off the infinitive, add *"o"* for *"yo"* and again, *"es"* for *"tú"*
Examples: infinitive: *escribir: Yo escrib-o, tú escrib-es*
          "   " *abrir: yo abr-o, tú abr-es*

☺ Extension Vocabulary: (corresponds to verb illustrations depicted on page 9d)
    hablar *(to talk, speak)*   **comer** *(to eat)*
    caminar *(to walk)*   **beber** *(to drink)*
    bailar *(to dance)*   **escribir** *(to write)* [not illustrated]
    mirar *(to look)*   **tocar** *(to touch or play an instrument)*

Extension Games and Activities:

A. Verb Vocabulary Cards
Practice the target and extension words with the verb vocabulary words on page 9d. Copy and cut a page for each student so that everyone has their own deck of verb cards. Give students simple *TPR commands to identify and practice the verbs, for example: *Toca el verbo "cantar".*   *Pon "nadar" en la cabeza.*
        Camina con "caminar".   *Pon "pintar" en tu zapato.*
        Párate con "beber".   *Dame "bailar".*
        Siéntate con "tocar".   *Dale "leer" a tu amigo.*
TPR commands are fully explained on introductory pages vii and viii of this book.

B. **Exotic Secret Verb Flowers**
   1) Distribute a paper plate, colors and scissors to each student.
   2) Instruct them to make their Exotic Secret Verb Flowers by cutting eight incisions into the paper plate, as shown by the dotted lines in the example to the left. They fold each of the eight flaps in and crease the fold to create petals.

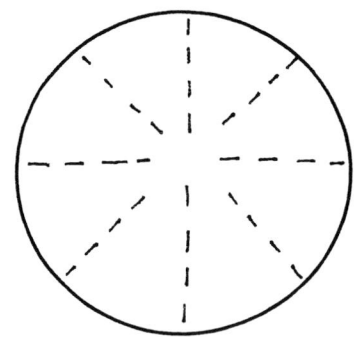

   3) Now they unfold the flower and on every petal they draw a stick figure of an action verb, and also write down the verb word. In the center of the flower, each student writes a secret or a wish – in Spanish of course.
   4) Collect the flowers. Shuffle and redistribute them so that no one has his own.
   5) Each student has a turn to present his Exotic Secret Verb Flower. He acts out the verb on each flap, giving the other students time to identify the word. Last of all, he reads the secret in the middle of the flower, and the class tries to identify the creator of that flower. After the creator is identified, he gets his flower back to keep.
   Note: Instruct students to only write secrets they don't mind their classmates hearing!

C. **¡Soy el Rey!** *("I am your King!")*
   All students stand in a circle. One student is "it" and loudly proclaims, *"Soy el Rey!"* ("I am the King!") – or *"Soy la Reina"* ("I am the Queen!") if "it" is a girl. The King then points around the circle to one classmate at a time, telling each what to do. (For example: *"Tú cantas. Tú pintas. Tú bailas. Tú nadas..."* etc.) The King may also gives himself something to do if he so wishes, i.e. *"Yo nado."* Each classmate, as he receives his task, repeats it in *"yo"* form and performs the action, continuing until everyone in the circle is doing something. The King then commands, *"¡Alto!"* (Stop!) He imperially commands someone to leave the circle, saying, *"[student's name] ¡Sal del reino!"* (Leave the kingdom!) That student leaves the circle and sits down. El Rey then chooses a new King, and the game continues, as the circle slowly becomes smaller and smaller.
   Note: The King may add direct objects to the sentence, i.e. *"Tú cantas una cancion. Tú nadas en el baño. Tú pintas un perro. Tú tocas la guitarra..."* and so on.

Make it Meaningful

Have students complete the Activity Sheet on page 9e according to their own lives and perceptions. Encourage them to answer truthfully and to add prepositional *phrases(i.e. "Yo canto en el baño."* or direct objects, *(i.e. "Yo canto una cancion del radio.")* to make their sentences more factual and interesting. Share and discuss answers.

The Song as a Teaching Tool

This song has great choreography! In pairs, students face each other.
Lyrics: *"¡Vamos a cantar! (Yo canto, tú cantas)"* 2X – While acting out the verb motion, students sway forward and back.
   "La cabeza, la cintura, el corazon, pon las manos en cada rodilla" – Execute these actions, still facing each other
   "¡Vamos a cantar! (Yo canto, tú cantas)" – Repeat swaying movements from beginning
   "Hasta la hora de cenar" – Fold arms and do-si-do around your partner
   Last three beats of music in verse – Slap knees, clap hands, and snap fingers

9. ¡Vamos a cantar! (Yo canto, tú cantas)

1. ¡Vamos a cantar! (Yo canto, tú cantas) (2X)
   ¡Vamos a cantar! (Yo canto, tú cantas) (2X)
   La cabeza, la cintura, el corazón
   Pon las manos en cada rodilla
   ¡Vamos a cantar! (Yo canto, tú cantas)
   Hasta la hora de cenar

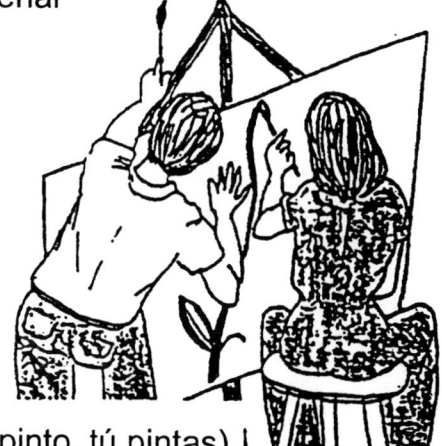

2. ¡Vamos a pintar! (Yo pinto, tú pintas)

3. ¡Vamos a nadar! (Yo nado, tú nadas)

4. ¡Vamos a leer! (Yo leo, tú tees)

5. ¡Vamos a jugar! (Yo juego, tú juegas)

9. ¡Vamos a cantar! (Yo canto, tú cantas)

See page 9b for game and activity ideas using these vocabulary cards.

9d

10. Yo prefiero México

Words and music by Patti Lozano

Muchos paises tienen islas y playas
Y montañas que besan el mar
Otros paises tienen ríos y lagos
Escondidos en la selva tropical

Estribillo:
　Muchos paises son interesantes
　　Cada con su sabor particular
　Mi corazón tiene un favorito
　There's just one place I wanna go
　Yo prefiero México.

2.　En Russia siempre hace frío
　　En España hace calor
　　En Inglaterra está lloviendo
　　¡Es fantástico viajar!

3.　En España comen el calamari
　　En Perú el cuey es especial
　　En Argentina comen el churrasco
　　Hay tanto que ver y probar

4.　México tiene islas y playas
　　Y montañas que besan el mar
　　México tiene ríos y lagos
　　Escondidos en la selva tropical

Many countries have islands and beaches
And mountains that kiss the sea
Other countries have rivers and lakes
Hidden in the tropical jungle (rainforest)

Refrain:
　Many countries are interesting
　Each with it's particular flavor
　My heart has one favorite
　There's just one place I wanna go
　I prefer Mexico

2. In Russia it's always cold
　In Spain it's hot
　In England it's raining
　It's fantastic to travel!

3. In Spain they eat "calamari" [squid]
　In Peru guinea pig is a specialty
　In Argentina they eat "el churrasco" [grilled meats]
　There's so much to try (taste)

4. Many countries have islands and beaches
　And mountains that kiss the sea
　Other countries have rivers and lakes
　Hidden in the tropical jungle (rainforest)

10. Yo prefiero México
Teaching Suggestions

Language Objectives: Topographical Terms
- ☺ Vocabulary: *(in order of appearance in the song)*
    - **el país** *(country)*
    - **la isla** *(island)*
    - **la playa** *(beach)*
    - **la montaña** *(mountain)*
    - **el mar** *(ocean, sea)*
    - **el río** *(river)*
    - **la selva tropical** *(tropical rainforest)*
    - **el lago** *(lake)*

- ☺ Cultural Notes: This geographical song is also a cultural lesson. Verse #3 names specific culinary specialties especially popular in some Spanish-speaking countries. They are:
  Calamari, which is squid and may be sauteed, or breaded and fried. It used to be a delicacy primarily in Spain and Greece, but now it is quite popular in the U.S.A. too.
  Cuey, which is guinea pig, and it's a favorite in Peru. In fact, hanging in the cathedral of the main square in Cuzco, is a painting of the Last Supper. The meal on the plate in front of Jesus is... yes, cuey.
  Churrasco, which is best known in Argentina and Uruguay, is a thick grilled steak, usually seasoned with *chimichurri*, a sauce made of olive oil, parsley and spices.

- ☺ Extension Vocabulary: (More topographical terms)
    - **el bosque** *(forest, woods)*   **la peninsula** *(peninsula)*
    - **la colina** *(hill)*   **el valle** *(valley)*
    - **la cascada** *(waterfall)*   **el volcán** *(volcano)*
    - **el desierto** *(desert)*   **la costa** *(the coast)*

Extension Games and Activities:

A. **What's in a Place?**
   Ask each student to bring a map of a favorite country or state. Have them circle and label mountains, beaches, lakes, rivers, etc.

B. **Planning a Road Trip**
   Using maps once again, have each student plan a week-long trip through a favorite country or state, outlining the route with a marker and sticking stars on special sights and stops. Share them and have students vote on the most exciting trip.

C. **Planning a Fantasy Trip**
   On the board or a large sheet of butcher paper, have students create the country... or planet. Have each student contribute, giving fantastical names and qualities to the land forms. Add some odd inhabitants and weather. Think Star Wars™ creativity!

D. **Canto de la geografía** *(Geography Chant)*

This simple rap/chant focuses on land forms. Chant it in a "swing" style. Devise gestures for the land forms and descriptions. Page 10d is the illustrated chant for students.

Del lago al río	From the lake to the river
Donde hace mucho frío;	Where it's very cold;
Del valle al mar	From the valley to the sea
Donde yo quiero nadar;	Where I want to swim;
Del bosque a la colina	From the forest to the hill
Donde vuele la golondrina;	Where the swallow flies;
Del volcán a la playa	From the volcano to the beach
Donde la vieja se desmaya,	Where the old lady faints;
Hasta la selva tan gigante	To the giant jungle
¡Para comer un chile picante!	To eat a hot pepper!

Guanajuato, Coahuila, Puebla, Chiapas, Michoacán,   [These are the names of 8 of
Sinaloa, Veracruz, ¡Ay Chihuahua! Yucatán   Mexico's 31 states]
(Say 3 times, first in a whisper, then with a regular voice, then as a yell!)

★Variations:
1) Once students know the rhyme well, stay silent on nouns and make hand gestures.
2) Split the class into two groups; one chants the odd lines and the other chants the even ones.
3) Try chanting the lines with different emotions.

Make it Meaningful

A. Have students bring and share vacation or scout trip photos. Every photo must have a topographical relevance, whether natural or man-made!

B. Ask students to think of their favorite food, hobby or sport. Now they must research to see how this food, hobby or sport is presented and/or modified in the Spanish-speaking country of their choice. They take turns to report their findings to the class (in English if necessary).

The Song as a Teaching Tool

Chant the lyrics to the song instead of singing it. After each topographical noun is spoken, pause to give students turns to call out sentences naming specific land forms in specific places. For example:
   Chanted: *Muchos países tienen islas...* [¡Cozumel es una isla! ¡Galveston es una isla!]
               y playas... [¡Destin tiene una playa! Rehoboth tiene una playa!]
               y montañas que besan el mar... [¡Hawaii tiene montañas que besan el mar!]
               Otros paices [Canadá es un país!] *tienen ríos...* [Brasil tiene un río!
               ¡Mississippi tiene un río muy largo!] ... and so on.
Notes: Let several students call out examples before continuing on with the chant.
★Variation: Make each student responsible for identifying land forms in a different country. Each student must have a map of his country at his disposal.

10. Yo prefiero México

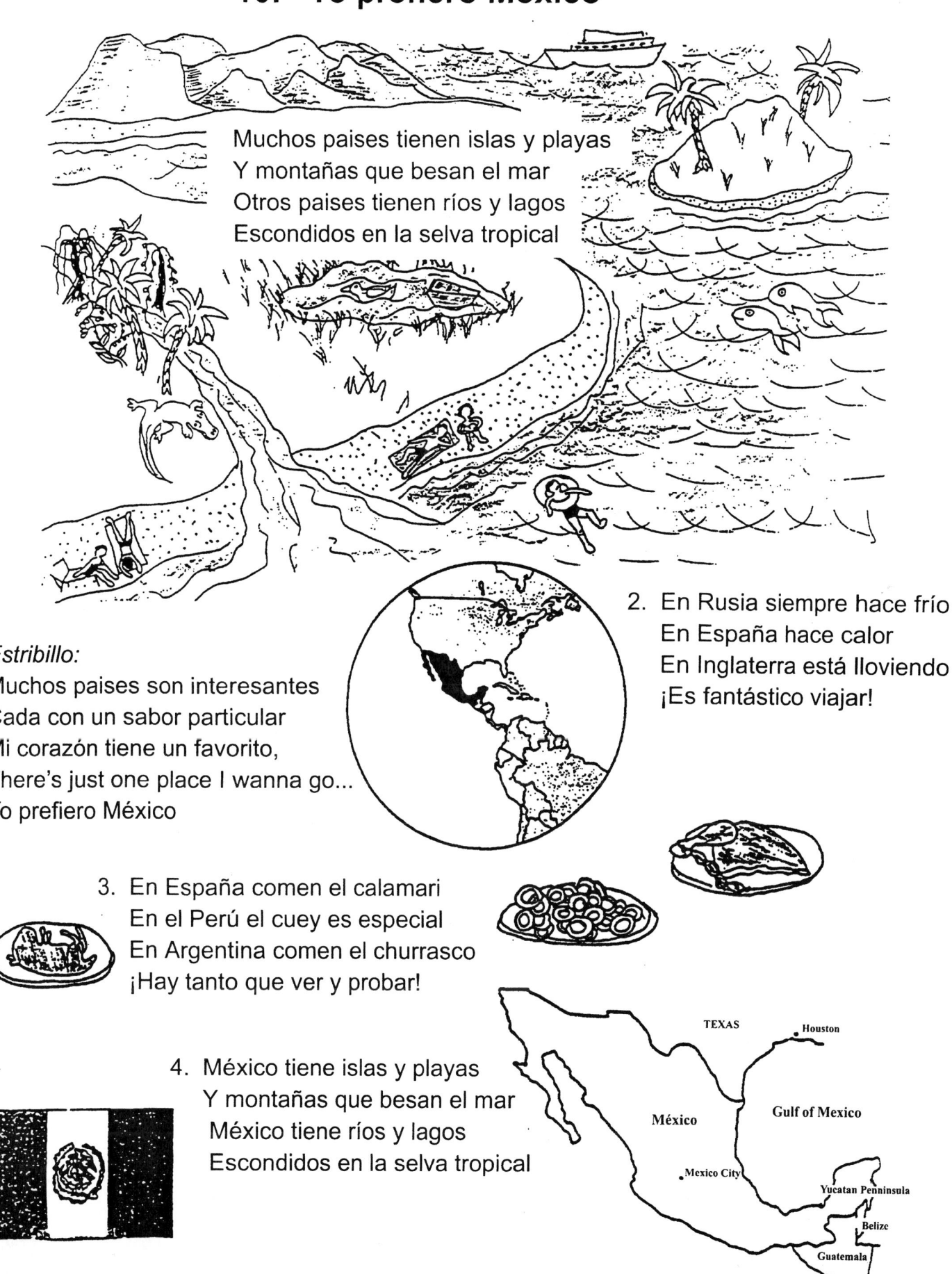

Muchos paises tienen islas y playas
Y montañas que besan el mar
Otros paises tienen ríos y lagos
Escondidos en la selva tropical

Estribillo:
Muchos paises son interesantes
Cada con un sabor particular
Mi corazón tiene un favorito,
There's just one place I wanna go...
Yo prefiero México

2. En Rusia siempre hace frío
   En España hace calor
   En Inglaterra está lloviendo
   ¡Es fantástico viajar!

3. En España comen el calamari
   En el Perú el cuey es especial
   En Argentina comen el churrasco
   ¡Hay tanto que ver y probar!

4. México tiene islas y playas
   Y montañas que besan el mar
   México tiene ríos y lagos
   Escondidos en la selva tropical

10. Yo prefiero México

Canto de la geografía de México

Del lago al río

Donde hace mucho frío;

Del valle al mar

Donde yo quiero nadar;

Del bosque a la colina

Donde vuele la golondrina;

Del volcán a la playa

Donde la vieja se desmaya,

¡Hasta la selva tan gigante

Para comer el chile picante!

¡Guanajuato, Coahuila, Puebla, Chiapas, Michoacán,
Sinaloa, Veracruz, ¡Ay, Chihuahua! Yucatán!

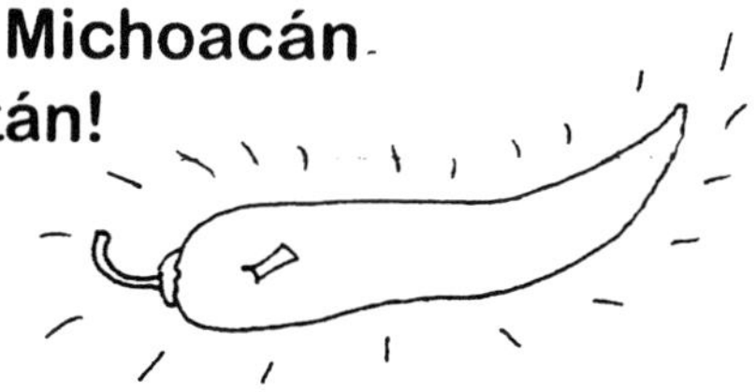

11. Leonor, mi amor, por favor

Words and music by Patti Lozano

Muchachos: (Estribillo)
Leonor, mi amor, por favor
Acompáñame al cine esta noche,
Y después comeremos
   tacos al carbon, con papas,
Leonor, mi amor, por favor

Muchachas: (Versos)
1. ¡Ay, mi Federico!
   No puedo aceptar tu invitación
   Pero làvate la cara y quizás
   Yo te puedo aguantar mejor

2. Péinate el pelo
3. Cepíllate los dientes
4. Cambia los zapatos
5. Plancha la camisa

Boys: (Refrain)
Leonor, my love, please
Accompany me to the movies tonight
And afterwards we'll eat
   tacos al carbon, with potatoes
Leonor, my love, please

Girls: (Verses)
1. Oh, my Frederick!
   I can't accept your invitation
   But wash your face and maybe
   I'll be able to tolerate you better

2. Comb your hair
3. Brush your teeth
4. Change your shoes
5. Iron your shirt

11. Leonor, mi amor, por favor
Teaching Suggestions

Language Objectives: Personal Hygiene and Command Verb Forms
- ☺ Vocabulary: *(in order of appearance in the song.)*
  - **Lávate la cara.** *(Wash your face.)*
  - **Péinate el pelo.** *(Comb your hair.)*
  - **Cepíllate los dientes.** *(Brush your teeth.)*
  - **Cambia los zapatos.** *(Change your shoes.)*
  - **Plancha la camisa.** *(Iron your shirt.)*

- ☺ Extension Vocabulary: (More commands, in order of appearance on page 11d)
  - **Cierra la puerta.** *(Close the door.)*
  - **Dibuja un triángulo.** *(Draw a triangle.)*
  - **Escribe tu nombre.** *(Write your name.)*
  - **Toma la flor.** *(Take the flower.)*
  - **Siéntate en la silla.** *(Sit in the chair.)*
  - **Ponte el sombrero.** *(Put on the hat.)*
  - **Come la manzana.** *(Eat the apple.)*
  - **Escucha la música.** *(Listen to the music.)*
  - **Toca la mesa.** *(Touch the table.)*
  - **Cuenta los dulces.** *(Count the candies.)*
  - **Canta una canción.** *(Sing a song.)*

Extension Games and Activities:

A. **Simón dice** *(Simon Says)*
Play *"Simón Dice"* (Simon Says) by using TPR commands with this unit's hygienic commands. Examples of commands:
   Simón dice –Lávate la cara. [Students mime washing their faces.]
   Simón dice –Cepíllate los dientes. [Students mime brushing their teeth.]
   Péinate el pelo. [Students do nothing because Simón didn't say it.]
When a student makes a mistake by performing the action although Simón didn't say to, he sits down. Continue until just a few "winners" are left standing. Add commands from the Extension Vocabulary list too.

B. **Human B-I-N-G-O**
Use the vocabulary cards on page 11d to play "Human BINGO". Distribute page 11d to half of the class. This is *Grupo Rojo* and they stand up. Give little star or dot stickers to the other half of the class. This is *Grupo Azul* and they stay seated.
The students in *Grupo Rojo* must complete to be the first to get a vertical, horizontal or diagonal row of stickers on their page. A *Grupo Rojo* student gets a sticker by walking to any seated *Grupo Azul* student, pointing to a vocabulary card and saying the correct command, at which point the *Grupo Azul* student places a sticker on that vocabulary card. A *seated* student may not be approached by a standing student more than once. The winning *Grupo Rojo* student gets a small prize. Then switch so that the *Grupo Azul* students seek stickers from the *Grupo Rojo* students.

C. **Carrera de mandatos** *(Race of Commands)*
   Everyone writes down five commands on paper. Divide the class into two teams. Student A from each team stands in front of his team and issues his five commands to five different students. As soon as his commands are executed, Student B stands and issues his five commands. The first team to finish all commands wins.

Make it Meaningful

Pairs of Scriptwriters
Pair students and instruct them to write a short skit based on the tribulations of Federico and Leonor. Give them time to rehearse. Later, let each group perform for the others. Don't worry if two boys or two girls are paired together. It's much more entertaining for the audience when a boy wears a girl's wig, or a girl wears a mustache.
Note: Scripts may be very short and simple, for example:
   Federico: Buenos días, Leonor.
   Leonor: Buenos días, Federico.
   Federico: Por favor, Leonor. Acompáñame al cine esta noche. Vamos a ver "Lord of the Rings".
   Leonor: No. No quiero ir al cine contigo.
   Federico: ¿Por que no?
   Leonor: Tu pelo está sucio. Lávate el pelo y quizás...
   Federico: ¡Gracias! Hasta luego.
   Leonor: Hasta luego, Federico.

The Song as a Teaching Tool

A. The boys sing Federico's lines and the girls sing Leonor's lines. Choose one boy and girl to act out the roles of the haughty Leonor and the sloppy Federico.

B. Sing the song cumulatively: on the first verse, just sing, *"Pero lávate la cara y quizás..."* After the Federico's next chorus, Leonor's lines instruct him to, *"Péinate tu pelo... y lávate la cara y quizás..."* By the fifth chorus, sing all five hygienic improvements Federico must make in order to have the honor of Leonor's company.

C. Add gestures to the above cumulative activity.

D. This song is a partner song! Both parts have the same chord structure and may be sung together for lovely counterpoint harmony. (The "Just Music!" CD, which is sold separately, has the instrumental accompaniment to the song without vocals, which makes this harmony sound especially nice!)

E. Think of additional verses, perhaps for older students and characters, such as:
   ...pero limpia tu coche y quizás... (... but clean out your car and maybe...)
   ...pero aféitate la barba y quizás... (... shave your beard and maybe....)

11. Leonor, mi amor, por favor

Estribillo: (muchachos)
Leonor, mi amor, por favor
Acompáñame al cine esta noche
Y después comeremos tacos al carbón - con papas
Leonor, mi amor, por favor

Versos: (muchachas)
¡Ay, mi Federico!
No puedo aceptar tu invitación,
Pero lávate la cara y quizás
Yo te podré aguantar mejor

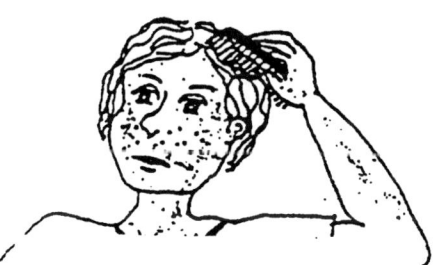

2. Péinate el pelo

3. Cepíllate los dientes...

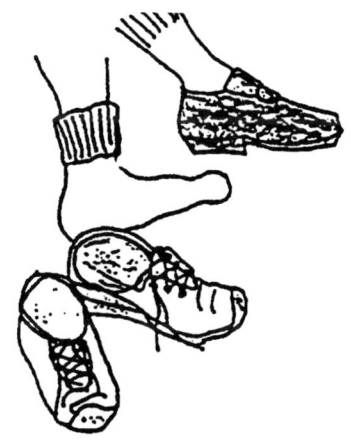

4. Cambia los zapatos...

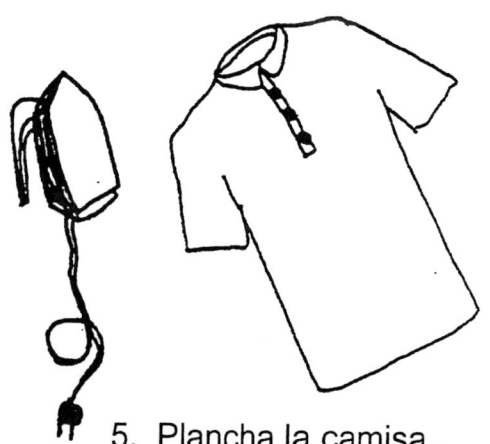

5. Plancha la camisa...

11. Leonor, mi amor, por favor
"Human BINGO"

See page 11b for instructions on how to use this gameboard.

Commands Used in this Game (in no particular order):

Lávate la cara.
Toca la flauta.
Cepíllate los dientes.
Cambia los zapatos
Lee el libro.
Ponte el sombrero.
Besa al perrito.
Habla por teléfono.

Plancha la camisa.
Dibuja el triángulo.
Mira al pájaro.
Levanta la mano.
Escribe tu nombre.
Cuenta los dulces.
Lee tu libro.

Cierra la puerta.
Siéntate en la silla.
Canta una canción.
Bebe el agua.
Come la manzana.
Toca la mesa.
Nada rápido.
Toma la flor.

12. Dos elefantes

Words and music by Patti Lozano

Estribillo:
  Dos elefantes escondidos en la selva
  En un día de agosto cuando hace calor
  El más grande de los elefantes dice muy triste –
  "¿Qué quieres hacer? ¿Qué quieres hacer?
  ¿Qué quieres hacer tú?"
  Y le dice –

1. Quiero ver la televisión
   En la selva no quiero estar hoy
   Quiero ver la televisión
   En el pueblo - ¡adiós, me voy!"

2. Quiero escuchar el radio...
3. Quiero escribir en la computadora...
4. Quiero jugar con carritos y muñecas...

Refrain:
  Two elephants hidden in the jungle
  One day in August when it's hot
  The biggest of the elephants says very sadly –
  What do you want to do? What do you want to do?
  What do you want to do?
  And he tells him –

1. "I want to watch television
    In the jungle   I don't want to be today
    I want to watch television
    In the town   - goodbye, I'm going!"

2. I want to listen to the radio...
3. I want to write on the computer...
4. I want to play with cars and dolls...

12a

12. Dos elefantes
Teaching Suggestions

Language Objectives: Leisure-time Activities, the verb *"querer"*

☺ Vocabulary: *(in order of appearance in the song)*
  ver la televisión *(watch television)*
  escribir en la computadora *(write on the computer)*
  escuchar el radio *(listen to the radio)*
  jugar con carritos y muñecas *(play with cars and dolls)*

☺ Structures: the verb *"querer"* [to like, to love, to want to]
  ¿Qué quieres hacer? *(What do you want to do?)*
  Quiero + verb... *(I want to + verb...)*

☺ Extension Vocabulary:
  Quiero tocar el piano. *(I want to play the piano.)*
  Quiero jugar al béisbol. *(I want to play baseball.)*
  Quiero dormir. *(I want to sleep.)*
  Quiero ir de compras con mis amigas. *(I want to go shopping with my friends.)*
  Quiero viajar. *(I want to travel.)*
  Quiero ir al cine. *(I want to go to the movies.)*
  Quiero comer en un restaurante. *(I want to eat in a restaurant.)*
  Quiero hablar por teléfono. *(I want to talk on the phone.)*

Extension Games and Activities:

A. Create **Silly Sentences** with the leisure activity vocabulary cards on page 12d, as well as the vocabulary cards on pages 1d (city places), 2f (rooms) and 7d (transportation). Give one full deck of cards to each student. The 12d (*"Yo quiero..."*) cards are placed face down in one pile, and the 1d, 2f and 7d (places) cards are placed in a second pile, also face down. Students now are able to create whimsical random sentences by linking a card from each pile, i.e. *"Yo quiero viajar"* might be linked with *"en el jardín."* More examples of random sentences: *"Yo quiero escuchar al radio... en mi bicicleta." "Yo quiero dormir... en el banco."*

B. **Silly Sentences in Role-Play Situations**
   To make a delightful paired role-playing activity with the above activity:
   1) Place students in groups of fours. For purposes of explanation, let's call one pair of students *"Verde A and Verde B,"* and the other pair *"Rojo A and Rojo B"*.
   2) *Verde A* faces *Rojo A*. *Verde A* chooses a card from both the page 12d *"Yo quiero..."* deck and the random 1d, 2f and 7d *"places"* deck and says the silly sentence to *Rojo A*. *Verde B* listens to his partner read, (he may NOT read the cards; his must listen) and, with total seriousness, acts out this ridiculous sentence to *Rojo B*. Remove these two cards from the remainder of the decks.
   3) Now switch so that *Rojo A* reads to *Verde A*, and *Rojo B* then acts out the sentence for *Verde A*.
   4) Continue until all cards have been played.

C. Un poema para el sábado

Enjoy the following rhyme (also featured on page 12e.) Have a Group A say the first line of the couplet, and a Group say the second while acting it out. The English translation is on the right.

Es la una de la tarde. ¿Qué quieres hacer?	It's 1:00 in the afternoon. What do you want to do?
Tengo mucho hambre y quiero comer.	I'm very hungry and I want to eat.
Son las dos de la tarde. ¿Qué quieres hacer?	It's 2:00 in the afternoon. What do you want to do?
Quiero jugar al fútbol y no quiero perder	I want to play soccer and I don't want to lose.
Son las tres de la tarde. ¿Qué quieres hacer?	It's 3:00...
Tengo un helado que te quiero ofrecer.	I have an ice cream that I want to offer you.
Son las cuatro de la tarde. ¿Qué quieres hacer?	It's 4:00...
Quiero comprar un libro porque quiero leer.	I want to buy a book because I want to read.
Son las cinco de la tarde. ¿Qué quieres hacer?	It's 5:00.....
Quiero tomar leche porque quiero crecer.	I want to drink milk because I want to grow.
Son las seis de la tarde. ¿Qué quieres hacer?	It's 6:00...
Quiero bailar con una linda mujer.	I want to dance with a pretty woman.
Son las siete de la tarde. ¿Qué quieres hacer?	It's 7:00...
Quiero ir a casa porque va a llover.	I want to go home because it's going to rain.
Son las ocho de la tarde. ¿A dónde quieres ir?	It's 8:00....
Pues, ahora es la noche y yo me quiero dormir.	Well, it's nighttime now and I want to go to sleep.
Pues, ahora es la noche y yo me quiero dormir.	Well, it's nighttime now and I want to go to sleep.

Make it Meaningful

Scriptwriters
Pair students and have them write a short skit based on one of these three scenarios:
1) A teenager babysits for three outspoken children. She has suggestions for what they may want to do, but they have their own ideas.
2) Two friends are bored on a rainy weekend. The optimistic friend has many good ideas, but the pessimistic friend shoots them all down.
3) Federico and Leonor are back from the previous song! Federico wants to take Leonor out and suggests so many wonderful possibilities, but Leonor prefers to do just about anything – as long as Federico is not there.

The Song as a Teaching Tool

As a class project, change the lyrics to *"Dos buen amigos aburridos en la sala..."* (Two good friends, bored in the livingroom....) Continue to revise the lyrics according to this theme.

12. Dos elefantes

Estribillo:
Dos elefantes escondidos en la selva
En un día de agosto cuando hace calor,
El más grande de los elefantes dice muy triste -
"¿Qué quieres hacer? ¿Qué quieres hacer?
¡Qué quieres hacer tú?"
Y le dice -

"Quiero ver la televisión.
En la selva no quiero estar hoy.
Quiero ver la televisión
En la selva. ¡Adiós, me voy!"

2. "Quiero escuchar el radio..."

3. "Quiero escribir en la computadora..."

4. "Quiero jugar con carritos y muñecas..."

12. Dos elefantes

See page 12b for game and activity ideas using these vocabulary cards.

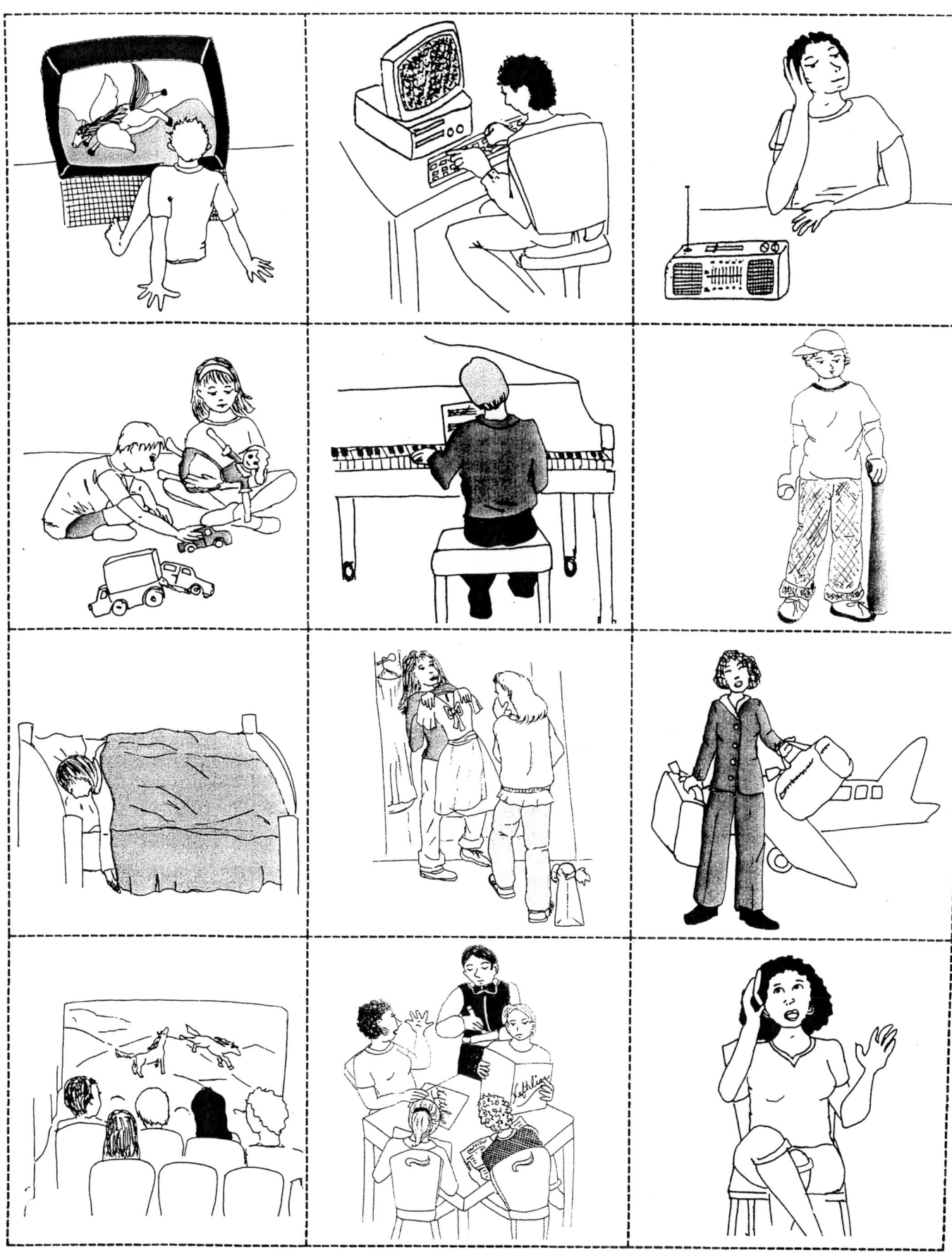

12d

12. Dos elefantes

Un poema para el sábado

Es la una de la tarde. ¿Qué quieres hacer?
Tengo mucho hambre y quiero comer.

Son las dos de la tarde. ¿Qué quieres hacer?
Quiero jugar al fútbol y no quiero perder.

Son las tres de la tarde. ¿Qué quieres hacer?
Tengo un helado que te quiero ofrecer.

Son las cuatro de la tarde. ¿Qué quieres hacer?
Quiero comprar un libro porque quiero leer.

Son las cinco de la tarde. ¿Qué quieres hacer?
Quiero tomar leche porque quiero crecer.

Son las seis de la tarde. ¿Qué quieres hacer?
Quiero bailar con una linda mujer.

Son las siete de la tarde. ¿Qué quieres hacer?
Quiero ir a casa porque va a llover.

Son las ocho de la tarde. ¿A dónde quieres ir?
Pues, ahora el la noche y yo me quiero dormir.
Pues, ahora es la noche y yo me quiero dormir.

13. O águila, escúchame

Words and music by Patti Lozano

[Musical notation with chords: Em D Em D G C / Em D Em D G Bsus4 B7 / C G / C G G#dim7 Am7 B7]

Lyrics under music:
O á-gui-la, es-cú-cha-me, y di-me de tus vi-a-jes. O á-gui-la, es-cú-cha-me, y di-me de tus vi-a-jes. Di-me del cam-po ver-de a-ba-jo con co-li-na tras co-li-na. Di-me de co-ne-jos, ra-to-nes y cu-le-bras y el puer-co-es-pín, ya

Estribillo:
O águila, escúchame y dime de tus viajes (2X)

Refrain:
Oh eagle, listen to me, and tell me of your journeys (2X)

Versos:
1. Dime del campo verde abajo
   Con colina tras colina
   Dime de conejos, ratones y culebras
   Y el puercoespín ya

2. Dime de árboles altos y viejos
   Hasta el cielo creciendo
   Dime de ardillas contentas en familias
   En los troncos viviendo

3. Dime de hermosas pequeñas mariposas
   En las flores descansando
   Dime de las filas de tantas hormigas
   Que siempre están marchando

4. Dime del muchacho sólo parado -
   Soy yo - te estoy mirando
   Quiero volar contigo por las nubes
   Nuestro mundo explorando

Verses:
1. Tell me of the green countryside below
   With hill after hill
   Tell me of rabbits, mice and snakes
   And the porcupine now

2. Tell me of tall, old trees
   Growing to the sky
   Tell me of squirrels happy in families
   Living in the tree trunks

3. Tell me of beautiful, little butterflies
   Resting on the flowers
   Tell me of the lines of so many ants
   That are always marching

4. Tell me of the boy, standing alone
   That's me - I am watching you
   I want to fly with you through the clouds
   Exploring our world

13. O águila, escúchame
Teaching Suggestions

Language Objectives: Nature, Countryside

☺ Vocabulary:

la águila *(eagle)*	**el puercoespín** *(porcupine)*
tus viajes *(your travels)*	**el árbol** *(tree)*
el campo *(countryside, field)*	**la ardilla** *(squirrel)*
la colina *(hill)*	**el tronco** *(trunk of a tree)*
el conejo *(rabbit)*	**la flor** *(flower)*
la culebra *(snake)*	**el cielo** *(sky)*
el ratón *(mouse)*	**la mariposa** *(butterfly)*
la hormiga *(ant)*	**las nubes** *(clouds)*

☺ Structures: Commands

Escúchame. *(Listen to me.)*   **Dime.** *(Tell me.)*

☺ Incidental Structures: the progressive tense ("-ing" form)
Rules: Verbs with infinitives ending in *"-ar"* become *"ando"*.
 Verbs with infinitives ending in *"-er"* or *"-ir"* become *"iendo"*. Examples:
 mirar (to look) becomes *"mirando"*   *vivir* (to live) becomes *"viviendo"*
Note: Usually the verb *"estar"* (to be) precedes the action verb, (i.e. *"Yo estoy cantando"* (I am singing) but this is not in the case in this song.
 IMPORTANT! The present tense should be understood very well before formally introducing the progressive tense! It is purely incidental in this song!
Progressive tense verbs in this song:
creciendo *(growing)* - from the verb *"crecer"* (to grow)
viviendo *(living)* - from the verb *"vivir"* (to live)
descansando *(resting)* - from the verb *"descansar"* (to rest)
marchando *(marching)* from the verb *"marchar"* (to march)
mirando *(looking)* from the verb *"mirar"* (to look, watch)
explorando *(exploring)* from the verb *"explorar"* (to explore)

☺ Extension Vocabulary:

la hierba *(grass)*	**el pato** *(duck)*
el bosque *(forest)*	**el sol** *(sun)*
la hoja *(leaf)*	**la lluvia** *(rain)*
la rama *(branch)*	**el venado** *(deer)*

Extension Games and Activities:

A. **Color Your World**
Get out those colors and bring the nature vocabulary cards to life! You may want to transfer and enlarge the cards on other pages, so that there are only 6 - 8 pictures on a page. Encourage students to draw additional animals and nature settings. Students may give the instructions. Examples: *"El águila mira el ratón. Hay dos ardillas en la rama del árbol. La mariposa es morada y azul. Hay una culebra cerca del venado. Un pájaro come la flor."* Use all of your review vocabulary from previous units!

B. **Postcards**

Obtain a class set of postcards of different landscapes. They may be old postcards from antique shops and secondhand stores, or fresh new postcards from souvenir shops and Wal-Marts around the world. Give each student a different postcard. (Photos from students' travels may also be used.) Here are some activities for them:

1) Have each student write a description of the view on the postcard, or on a separate postcard-sized piece of paper. Have them "mail" their postcard to another student in the class. Students take turns reading the postcards they received out loud and show the picture to the class. A very well-written postcard might say this:

   "Este es un lago grande en Oregon. Se llama Crater Lake. El agua
   es azul y es muy bonito. Hay muchos árboles cerca del lago.
   Las ardillas viven en los árboles. No hay nubes en el cielo."

2) Prepare descriptions of each postcard prior to handing them out to students. Students examine their postcards as you read a description. When you are completely finished, students raise their hands if they think you are describing their postcards. Go over the details together to identify the correct postcard holder.

C. **Utilizing Famous Paintings**

Make a transparency of a famous landscape painting, or a picture with people with an interesting landscape in the background - or place the painting from an art book on a doc cam. Project the image on a white board. Give students a number of people and animal cutouts, either from magazines or from vocabulary cards. You may also use pictures that they have drawn free-hand. Tell students where to place their cutouts in the landscape. Students stick them to the board with magnets, ticky tack or tape.

Instruction examples:

   La muchacha está a la derecha de la colina.
   La vaca está en el campo.

You may also distribute cutouts of this unit's target vocabulary to further reinforce the objectives, (i.e. *"Hay dos nubes en el cielo."*)

D. Choose a famous landscape that only you may see. Give students paper and colors. Describe the landscape, location of items and colors and students draw according to your description. Then show the print of the painting. Who drew the picture most similar to the famous artwork?

Make it Meaningful

Have student discuss where they would like to travel on their summer vacations and why. They may show travel brochures and describe photos if they wish

The Song as a Teaching Tool

Give each student a 2-foot long strip of white calculator paper. As you teach the target vocabulary words (in the order in which they appear in the song,) students draw pictures of each new noun and label each with the correct word. Then they roll their papers up, end-of-song first. Later, when the class sings the song through, students unroll their papers so that they have picture dictionaries of the lyrics they are singing. This is a good activity for songs with lots of new nouns. In subsequent renditions of the song, they may trade paper rolls with classmates to see different versions of the vocabulary words.

13. O águila, escúchame

Estribillo:
O águila, escúchame y dime de tus viajes
O águila, escúchame y dime de tus viajes

Versos:

1. Dime del campo verde abajo
   Con colina tras colina
   Dime de conejos, ratones y culebras
   Y el puercoespín ya

2. Dime de árboles altos y viejos
   Hasta el cielo creciendo
   Dime de ardillas contentas en familias
   En los troncos viviendo

3. Dime de hermosas pequeñas mariposas
   En las flores descansando
   Dime de las filas de tantas hormigas
   Que siempre están marchando

4. Dime del muchacho sólo parado,
   Soy yo, te estoy mirando
   Quiero volar contigo por las nubes
   Nuestro mundo explorando

13. O águila, escúchame

See page 13b for game and activity idas using these vocabulary cards.

13d

14. Hay que ir al zoológico

Words and music by Patti Lozano

1. No hay que viajar (a Africa)
   Para ver un tigre caminar
   No hay que viajar (a Canadá)
   Para ver un oso jugar
   No hay que viajar (a Ecuador)
   Para ver una foca nadar

Estribillo:
   Sólo hay que ir al zoológico
   Hay que ir al zoológico
   Para ver los animales de toda la tierras
   Hay que ir al zoológico

2. No hay que viajar   (a México)
   Para ver un loro cantar
   No hay que viajar   (a Australia)
   Para ver un canguro saltar
   No hay que viajar (a Asia)
   Para ver un mono gritar

3. No hay que viajar   (a India)
   Para ver un elefante pasar
   No hay que viajar (a Egipto)
   Para ver un camello masticar
   No hay que viajar (a Florida)
   Para ver un flamingo volar

1. It's not necessary to travel (to Africa)
   To see a tiger walk
   It's not necessary to travel (to Canada)
   To see a bear play
   It's not necessary to travel (To Ecuador)
   To see a seal swim

Refrain:
   You just have to go to the zoo
   You have to go to the zoo
   To see the animales from all of the lands
   You have to go to the zoo

2. It's not necessary to travel (to Mexico)
   To see an parrot sing
   It's not necessary to travel (to Australia)
   To see a kangaroo jump
   It's not necessary to travel (to Asia)
   To see a monkey scream

3. It's not necessary to travel (to India)
   To see an elephant pass by
   It's not necessary to travel (to Egypt)
   To see a camel chew
   It's not necessary to travel (to Florida)
   To see a flamingo fly

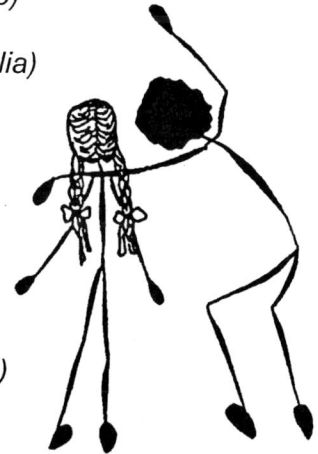

14. Hay que ir al zoológico
Teaching Suggestions

Language Objectives: Zoo Animals
- ☺ Vocabulary: (In order of appearance in song)

  Animals:
  - **el tigre** *(tiger)*
  - **el oso** *(bear)*
  - **la foca** *(seal)*
  - **el loro** *(parrot)*
  - **el canguro** *(kangaroo)*
  - **el mono** *(monkey)*
  - **el elefante** *(elephant)*
  - **el camello** *(camel)*
  - **el flamingo** *(flamingo)*

  Their actions:
  - **caminar** *(to walk)*
  - **jugar** *(to play)*
  - **nadar** *(to swim)*
  - **cantar** *(to sing)*
  - **saltar** *(to jump)*
  - **gritar** *(to scream)*
  - **pasar** *(to pass by)*
  - **masticar** *(to chew)*
  - **volar** *(to fly)*

- ☺ Structures: **Hay que...** *(It's necessary to...)*
  No hay que... *(It's not necessary to...)*
  Sólo que hay... *(It's only necessary to...)*

- ☺ Extension Vocabulary: (only words with * are illustrated on page 14d)
  - **el cocodrilo*** *(crocodile)*
  - **el jaguar** *(jaguar)*
  - **el armadillo** *(armadillo)*
  - **el mapache** *(raccoon)*
  - **el pingüino*** *(penguin)*
  - **el lobo** *(wolf)*
  - **la rana*** *(frog)*
  - **la jirafa** *(giraffe)*
  - **el hipopótamo** *(hippopotamus)*
  - **el león** *(lion)*
  - **la cebra** *(zebra)*
  - **el murciélago** *(bat)*

Note: Don't forget to use animal vocabulary from previous songs in this book: farm animals from *"El rancho de Pancho"*, iguanas from *"Las siete iguanas"*, sea animals from *"Cáscara de coco"* and field animals from *"O águila, escúchame"*.

Extension Games and Activities:

A. **Cube Game**
   1) Buy two small (approx 3 - 4") white square boxes from a shipping store. Label the six sides of one with colors: *rojo, negro, blanco, café, gris, verde*. Label the other with the following six attributes: *vive en el agua, vive en la tierra, come carne, come plantas, es grande, es pequeño*.
   2) Divide students into two teams.
   3) Student A on the A team rolls both cubes as dice. He reads the color and attribute on each side facing up, and receives a point for his team if he can name an animal that fulfills both the color and attribute. For example, if the cube lands on *"rojo"* and *"vive en el agua,"* he might say, *"el coral"* or *"el pez"* (from the review song, *"Cáscara de coco"*). The team with the highest number of points wins.
   ★Variation: If the student can also make a sentence about the habitat, country or behavior of the animal, he receives an extra point.

B. **Animal composite**
   Draw an imaginary animal on the board, asking each student to contribute a part of the body that fits one specific animal. For example: *"La cabeza es del loro; las orejas son del elefante; las piernas son del flamigo..."* etc. The result will be hilarious.
   ★Variation: Have each student draw a composite animal; the class figures out which body part comes from which animal.

C. **Chart Animal Characteristics**
   Create a chart to describe ten animals as featured in the figure below:

Animal	Color	Sonido *(Sound)*	Hábitat	País *(Country)*	Comida *(Food)*

D. **Who Am I?**
   Make one class set of 14d flashcards. Cut them apart and tape one to each student's forehead. They walk around asking other students questions until the figure out which animal they are. *(Examples: ¿Cómo plantas? ¿Soy pequeño? ¿Vivo donde hace frío?)*

Make it Meaningful

In small groups students draw a blueprint of the layout of the zoo in your city, i.e. buildings, habitats, large cages, etc. They draw and label the animal that lives in each area. (They may prefer to glue in pictures of the animals featured on the page 14d flashcards.)

The Song as a Teaching Tool

A. **World of Animals**

1) Display the World Map on page 14e on a transparency or doc cam.
2) Cut a page of the 14d animal flashcards apart and glue each one to a Post It™ note. Distribute these sticky note pages to students.
3) Singing the song: In the rhythmic break between the lyrics, *"No hay que viajar"* and *"para ver un _____"*, the student with that flashcard shouts out *"¡a África!"* – or to whichever continent is correct for the animal on their Post It Note™ and that line of the song. During the remainder of that song line, he affixes his animal to that continent, which is projected on to the board.

B. One final review! Review the animals from other songs and action verbs by creating additional verses, i.e. from *"O águila, escúchame"*: *"No hay que viajar para ver una hormiga marchar..."*

14. Hay que ir al zoológico

1. No hay que viajar (a Africa)
   Para ver un tigre caminar
   No hay que viajar (a Cánada)
   Para ver un oso jugar
   No hay que viajar (a Ecuador)
   Para ver una foca nadar
   Sólo hay que ir al zoológico,
   Hay que ir al zoológico
   Para ver los animales de todas las tierras
   Hay que ir al zoológico

2. No hay que viajar (a México)
   Para ver un loro cantar
   No hay que viajar (a Australia)
   Para ver un canguro saltar
   No hay que viajar (a Asia)
   Para ver un mono gritar
   Sólo hay que ir al zoológico
   Hay que ir al zoológico
   Para ver los aniamles de todas las tierras
   Hay que ir al zoológico

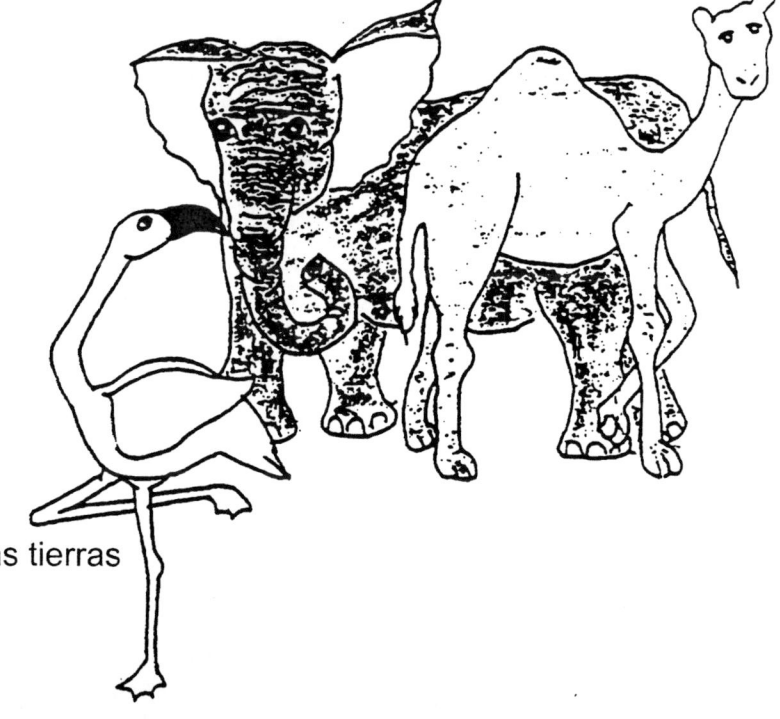

3. No hay que viajar (a India)
   Para ver un elefante pasar
   No hay que viajar (a Egipto)
   Para ver un camello masticar
   No hay que viajar (a Florida)
   Para ver un flamingo volar
   Sólo hay que ir al zoológico
   Hay que ir al zoológico
   Para ver los animales de todas las tierras
   Hay que ir al zoológico

14. Hay que ir al zoológico

See page 14b for game and activity ideas using these vocabulary cards.

14d

14. Hay que ir al zoológico

See page 14B for game and activity ideas for using this world map.

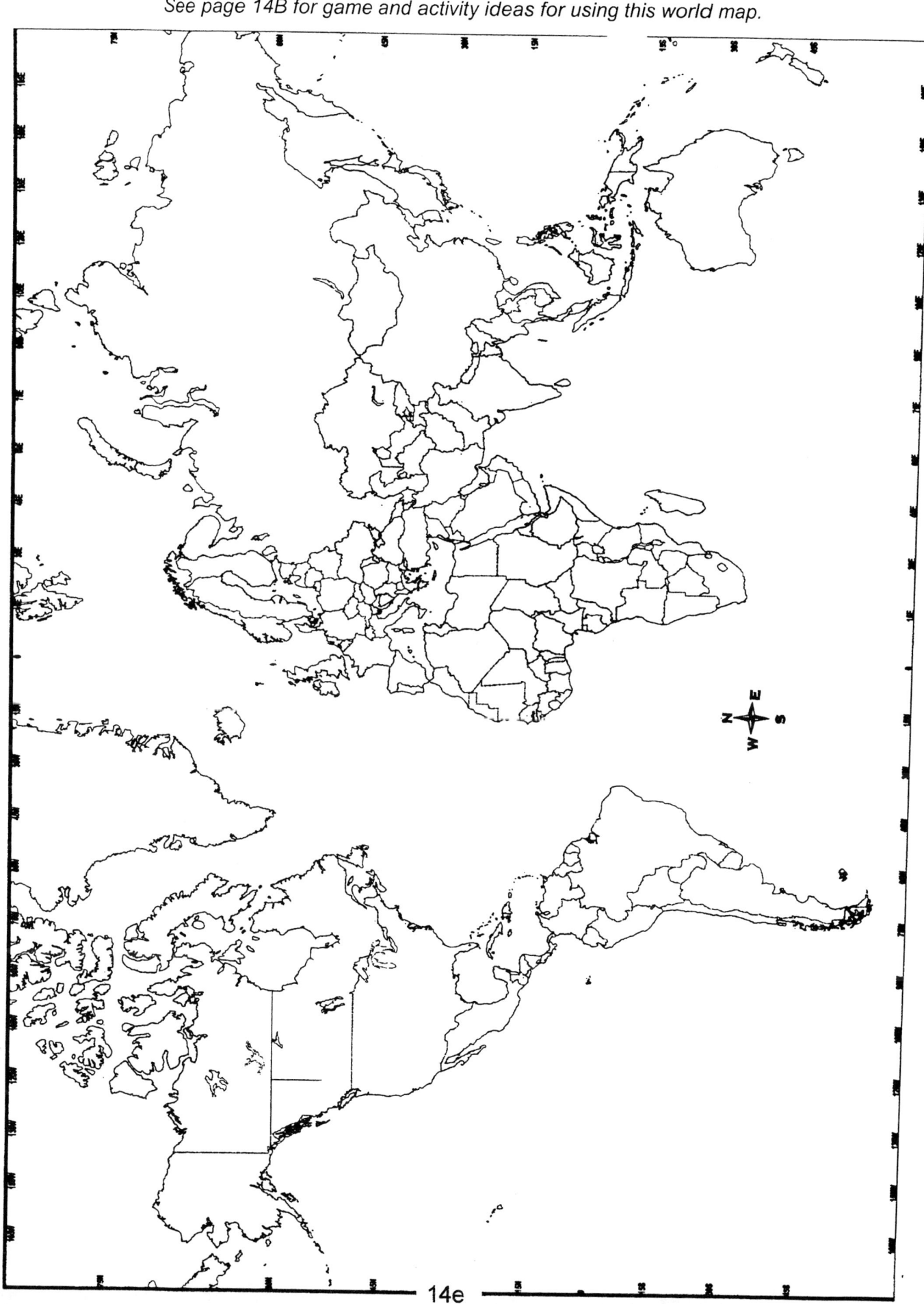

14e

Glossary

Spanish — English

Glossary
Spanish - English

A

a veces	sometimes
abajo	down
abuela, la	grandmother
abuelo, el	grandfather
aburrido(a)	bored
aceptar	to accept
adelante	forward
Aféitate la barba.	Shave your beard.
agosto	August
agua, el	water
aguantar	to tolerate
ahora	now
al lado de	by the side of
acciones, las	actions
Acompáñame.	Accompany me.
actriz, la	actress
adentro	inside
adentro (de)	inside of
al carbon	charcoal-grilled
alfombra, la	rug
alrededor	around
afuera	outside
amargo(a)	bitter
águila, la	eagle
allá	over there
alrededor	all around
alto(a)	tall
animales domesticados	pets
árbol, el	tree
ardilla, la	squirrel
arena, la	sand
armadillo, el	armadillo
arriba	up
así estoy contento	this way I'm happy
atacar	attack
autobús, el	bus
avión, el	airplane
azul	blue

B

bailar	to dance
bajo(a)	short
ballena, la	whale
banco, el	bank
baño, el	bathroom
barco, el	ship
bastante	enough, quite a lot
beber	to drink
béisbol, el	baseball
besar	to kiss
biblioteca, la	library
bicicleta, la	bicycle
bolsa, la	purse, bag
bonito(a)	pretty
bosque, el	forest
bueno(a)	good
buscan peces	look for fish

C

caballo, el	horse
cabeza, la	head
cacto, el	cactus
cada	each
calamari, el	squid
calle, la	street
cama, la	bed
camarón, el	shrimp
cambia	change
camisa, la	shirt
camello, el	camel
caminar	to walk
camión, el	truck
camioneta, la	minivan
campo, el	countryside, field
canción, la	song
cangrejo, el	crab
canguro, el	kangaroo
cantar	to sing
carritos, los	little (toy) cars
carta, la	letter
casa, la	house
cascada, la	waterfall
cáscara, la	shell (of a coconut)
cebra, la	zebra
cena, la	dinner
centro, el	downtown
Centroamérica	Central America

cepíllate	brush (ex. your teeth)
cerca de	near
cerdo, el	pig
chango, el	monkey
chimenea, la	chimney
chulo(a)	cute
churrasco, el	grilled meat dish (S.A.)
cielo, el	sky
Cierra la puerta.	Shut (close) the door.
cine, el	movie theater
cintura, la	waist
círculo, el	circle
ciudad, la	city
claro(a)	light, clear
clave, la	key
coche, el	automobile
cochino, el	pig
cocina, la	kitchen
coco, el	coconut
cocodrilo, el	crocodile
colina, la	hill
comedor, el	dining room
comer	to eat
comeremos	we will eat
cómico(a)	funny, comical
compañero(a)	companion
computadora, la	computer
concha, la	seashell
conejo, el	rabbit
contento(a)	happy
conmigo	with me
contigo	with you
coral, el	coral
corazón, el	heart
correo, el	mail
cortinas, las	curtains, drapes
corto(a)	short
costa, la	coast
crecer	to grow
creciendo	growing
cruza con al pierna	cross with the leg
cuadrado, el	square
cuey, el	cooked guinea pig
¿Cuál?	Which?
¿Cuántos?	How many?
cuarto, el	room
cuarto de recreo, el	playroom
Cuenta...	Count...
culebra, la	snake

D

Dale...	Give him/her...
Dame...	Give me...
de pie	on foot
debajo (de)	under
delante (de)	in front of
delfín, el	dolphin
delgado(a)	thin
derecha (a la)	(to the) right
descansando	resting
desierto, el	desert
después	after, afterwards
detrás (de)	behind
día, el	day
diamante, el	diamond
Dibuja...	Draw...
dibujar	to draw
dice	says
dientes, los	teeth
Dímelo	Tell it to me
dinero, el	money
dinosaurio, el	dinosaur
discos compactos, los	CDs
divertido(a)	fun
donde	where
dormitorio, el	bedroom
dormir	to sleep
dos	two
ducha, la	shower bath
dulces, los	candies
duro(a)	hard

E

edificios, los	buildings
Egipto	Egypt
elefante, el	elephant
elegante	elegant
en realidad	actually
enfermo(a)	sick, ill
ensalada, la	salad
entre	between
Es la una.	It's 1:00.
escondido(a)	hidden
escribir	to write
escritorio, el	desk
Escúchame.	Listen to me.
escuchar	to listen
España	Spain

especial	special	hacia	toward
Estados Unidos, los	United States	hamburguesa, la	hamburger
estante, el	bookcase	hasta	until
estrella del mar, la	starfish	Hasta luego.	Until later.
estrella, la	star	hay que...	It is necessary to...
estúpido(a)	stupid	hermana, la	sister
explorando	exploring	hermano, el	brother
		hierbas, las	grass, pasture
		hija, la	daughter
		hijo, el	son

F

familia, la	family
fantástico	fantastic
farmacia, la	pharmacy
favorito	favorite
feliz	happy, joyful
feo(a)	ugly
feroz (feroces)	fierce
fila, la	row, line, file
flamenco, el	flamingo
flamingo, el	flamingo
flauta, la	flute
flor, la	flower
flores, las	flowers
florero, el	flower vase
flotar	to float
foca, la	seal
fuera (de)	outside of
fútbol, el	football

hipopótamo, el	hippopotamus
hojas, las	leaves, pages
hormigas, las	ants
hospital, el	hospital
hotel, el	hotel

I

iguana, la	iguana
Inglaterra	England
inteligente	intelligent
interesante	interesting
invitación, la	invitation
ir	to go
ir de compras	to go shopping
isla, la	island
izquierda (a la)	(to the) left

J

jardín, el	garden
jaula, la	cage
joven	young
jugar	to play (a game)
jugo, el	juice
junto(s)	together

G

gallina, la	chicken, hen
gallo, el	rooster
garage, el	garage
gato, el	cat
gente, la	people
gigante	gigantic
globo, el	balloon
golondrina, la	swallow (bird)
gordo(a)	fat
grande	big
gritar	to scream
grupo, el	group

K

L

la __ más bonita	the prettiest __
la __ más delgada	the thinnest __
la __ más fea	the ugliest __
la __ más gorda	the fattest __
la __ más grande	the biggest
la __ más pequeña	the smallest
lago, el	lake
laguna, la	lagoon
lámpara, la	lamp

H

hablar	to talk, to speak
hace calor	it's hot
hace frío	it's cold
hacer	to do

largo(a)	long
Lávate la cara.	Wash your face.
leche, la	milk
leer	to read
lejos (de)	far from
leopardo, el	leopard
libro, el	book
limpio(a)	clean
lindo(a)	pretty
llama, la	llama
llave, la	key
lleno(a)	full, full of
lloviendo	raining
lo buscaré	I'll look for it
lobo, el	wolf
lodo, el	mud
loro, el	parrot

M

malo(a)	bad
manos, las	hands
manzana, la	apple
mapache, el	raccoon
mar, el	ocean
marchando	marching
mariposa, la	butterfly
masticar	to chew
mató (la mató)	he/she killed her
me quiero dormir	I want to go to sleep.
me voy	I'm going, I'm leaving
mediano(a)	medium
medicina, la	medicine
médico	doctor
medusa, la	jellyfish
mejor	better
mesa, la	table
mi amor	my love
¡Mira!	Look! Watch!
mirando	looking, watching
mono, el	monkey
montaña, la	mountain
motocicleta, la	motorcycle
mundo, el	world
mujer, la	lady
muñeca, la	doll
murciélago, el	bat (animal)
museo (de ciencias)	science museum
música, la	music

N

nadar	to swim
necesito	I need
nieve, la	snow, sherbet
No hay que...	It's not necessary to...
No importa	It doesn't matter
no quiero	I don't want to
No sé que hacer	I don't know what to do
noche, la	night
nombre, el	name
Norteamérica	North America
nubes, las	clouds
nuestro(a)	our
nuevo(a)	new
nunca	never

O

oficina, la	office
oficina del correo	post office
ofrecer	to offer
orejas, las	ears
oscuro(a)	dark
oso, el	bear
otro(s), otra(s)	other
oveja, la	sheep

P

país, el	country
paises, los	countries
pajarito, el	little bird
pájaro, el	bird
palacio, el	palace
palmeras, las	palm trees
palomitas, las	popcorn
pan, el	bread
pantalones, los	pants
papas fritas, las	french fries
parado	standing
Párate.	Stand up.
parece	to look like
pasar	to pass by
pasos adelante	forward steps
pasos atrás	backward steps
patio, el	patio
pato, el	duck
Péinate el pelo	Comb your hair
península, la	peninsula

pequeño(a)	small, little
perder	to lose
perdido(a)	lost
perico, el	parrot
perro, el	dog
pez, el	fish
picante	spicy
pingüino, el	penguin
pintar	to paint
piña, la	pineapple
piscina, la	swimming pool
pizza, la	pizza
planchar	to iron
plátanos, los	bananas
planta, la	plant
playa, la	beach
pollo, el	chicken (cooked)
Pon...	Put...
Ponte...	Put on...
popote, el	drinking straw (Mex.)
por favor	please
prefiero	I prefer
probar	to try, to taste
pueblo, el	town, village
puede	can
no puede	can't
puercoespín, el	porcupine
puerta, la	door
pues	well
pulpo, el	octopus

Q

¿Qué paso?	What happened?
¿Qué quieres hacer?	What do you want to do?
Quiero ver...	I want to see...
Quiero viajar...	I want to travel...
quizás	maybe

R

rama, la	branch
rana, la	frog
rancho, el	ranch, farm
ratón, el	rat
ratoncito, el	mouse
recreos pasatiempos, los	leisure activities
rectángulo, el	rectangle
refrigerador, el	refrigerator
reina, la	queen
restaurante, el	restaurant
revista, la	magazine
rey, el	king
río, el	river
rodilla, la	knee
ropa, la	clothing

S

sábado, el	Saturday
saber	to know
sabor, el	flavor
¡Sal del reino!	Leave the kingdom!
sala, la	living room
saltar	to jump
sano(a)	healthy
se desmaya	(he/she) faints
se esconde	(he/she/it) hides
se fué	(he/she/it) went
se quedó	(he/she/it) stayed
selva, la	jungle
selva tropical, la	tropical rainforest
serio(a)	serious
sentarse	to sit
siempre	always
Siéntate.	Sit down.
silla, la	chair
sobre	over
sobre, el	envelope
sofá, el	sofa, couch
sólo	alone
sólo hay que	it's only necessary to
sombrero, el	hat
Son las dos, tres...	It's 2:00, 3:00...
sordo(a)	deaf
soy	I am
suave	soft
subió	(he/she/it) climbed
sucio(a)	dirty
Sudamérica	South America
supermercado, el	supermarket

T

tarde, la	afternoon
techo, el	roof
teléfono, el	telephone
Tengo mucho	I'm very hungry.

hambre.	
tiburón, el	shark
tienda (de ropa)	(clothing) store
tierras, las	lands
tigre, el	tiger
tímido(a)	timid, shy
tío, el	uncle
tipo, el	type
toalla, la	towel
toca el sol	touch the sun
toca la tierra	touch the earth
tocar	to touch, to play
tocar el piano	to play the piano
tocar la guitarra	to play the guitar
todo/todos, toda/todas	all
todo el mundo	everybody, everyone
Toma...	Take...
tomar	to take, to drink
tomar el sol	to sunbathe
torta, la	cake
tortuga, la	turtle
trabajar	to work
transporte, el	transportation
tras	after
tren, el	train
triángulo, el	triangle
triste	sad
tronco, el	trunk (of a tree)
tú	you

U – V

va a llover	it's going to rain
vaca, la	cow
valle, el	valley
Vamos a...	Let's...
venado, el	deer
ventana, la	window
ver	to see
ver la televisión	watch television
verbos, los	verbs
verde	green
viajar	to travel
viajes, los	voyages, travels
vieja, la	the old woman
viejo(a)	old
viviendo	living
volar	to fly
volcán, el	volcano
volver pronto	return soon
Voy a(l)...	I'm going to the ...

W – X – Y – Z

ya	now
yo	I
Yo canto, tú cantas	I sing, you sing
Yo juego, tú juegas	I play, you play
Yo leo, tú lees	I read, you read
Yo nado, tú nadas	I swim, you swim
zapatos, los	shoes
¡Zas!	[An exclamation}
zoológico, el	zoo

RULES FOR PRONOUNCING ANY SPANISH WORD

1. Spanish is a phonetic language; that means that you always pronounce a Spanish word according to the way it is spelled. That also means that once you know how to pronounce a word you'll also know how to spell it.
2. Spanish vowels are sounded in this way: "a" = "ah"
   "e" = "ay"
   "i" = "ee"
   "o" = "oh"
   "u" = "oo"
3. Only 5 Spanish consonants are pronounced exactly the same way they are in English: "f," "l," "m," "n," and "q," The others can be a little tricky.

   "j" = "h"---- the Spanish word for juice is jugo; it is pronounced "hoogoh."
   "x"= a gargled sound, pronounced like an "h" with a bit of a "y" in front.
   "ll"= "y"----the Spanish word lleno means full; it is pronounced "yaynoh."
   "d"= a cross between a soft "d" and a "th" -- pronounced with the tip of the tongue touching the edge of the upper teeth.
   "g"= pronounced "guh" before "a," "o," "u," or before consonants; pronounced as "h" before "e" or "i."
   "b" and "v" = these two are pronounced in the same way: a very soft "b" pronounced with the edge of the upper teeth barely touching the lower lip.
   "h" = not pronounced---which means Spanish is not perfectly phonetic!
   "r" = pronounced but tap only once and very lightly with the tip of the tongue against the ridge in your mouth behind the upper teeth, like saying an "r" and a "d" at one time.
   "rr"= produced in the same way as "r" but with a minimum of 3 taps or rapid trills.
   "ch" = pronounced "tch" as in the English word watch.
   "ñ" = like "nyuh" but pronounced while the tip of the tongue is against the inside of the lower teeth ---- the Spanish word for tomorrow is mañana; it is a good one to practice on; pronounce it "mahnyuhahnah."
   "p," "t," & "k" = these are pronounced as in English, but without a puff of breath between the consonant and the following vowel.
   "s" = similar to "s" in English, but all "s" sounds in Spanish are pronounced with a very slight lisp caused by turning the tip of the tongue upwards as the sound is made.
   "c" = "s" when it comes before "e" or "i;"
      "k" = when it comes before "a," "o," "u," or consonants.
   "z" = "ss" ---- there is no "zz" sound in Spanish.
4. There are three simple rules for knowing which syllable is accented in any Spanish word.
   (a) Words ending in a vowel or in the consonants "n" or "s" are stressed on the next to last syllable. In a 2-syllable word, the accent would be on the first syllable; a 3-syllable word, the accent would be on the second.
      EXAMPLES: lunes (lú-nes) ---- the Spanish word for Monday
      sombrero (som-bré-ro) ---- the Spanish word for hat
   (b) Words ending in "ey," "oy," or "ay" or in any of the consonants other that "n" or "s" are stressed on the last syllable.
      EXAMPLES: verdad (ver-dád) ---- the Spanish word for truth
      comer (co-mér) ----- the Spanish verb meaning to eat
   (c) When the word is an exception to either of the two rules listed above, an accent should be written along with the word to show you where to place the stress.
      EXAMPLES: lápiz---- the Spanish word for pencil
      azúcar -- the Spanish word for sugar
      cortés --- the Spanish word for courtesy

Information and Order Page

Dolo Publications, Inc.
18315 Spruce Creek Drive
Houston, TX 77084
Email: dolo@wt.net

Tel. (281) 493-4552 or
(281) 463-6694
FAX (281) 679-9092
www.dololanguages.com

Send check, Charge, FAX or Purchase Order to above address, or Call Toll-Free 1-800-830-1460 to place an order.

Item No.	Description	Unit Price	Total
MS1	Music That Teaches Spanish - Book and CD	$31.95	
MM2	More Music That Teaches Spanish - Book and CD	$31.95	
ME5	Music That Teaches English - Book and CD	$31.95	
MF7	Music That Teaches French - Book and CD	$31.95	
MG9	Music That Teaches German - Book and CD	$31.95	
LC3	Leyendas con Canciones! - Book and CD & Activity Masters	$31.95	
LAL11	Latin-American Legends: On Page, on Stage and in Song - Book and CD	$31.95	
SGS8	Spanish Grammar Swings! - Book and CD	$31.95	
TCH10	Teatro de Cuentos de Hadas	$24.95	
PS4	Mighty Mini-Plays for the Spanish Classroom	$21.95	
PF4	Mighty Mini-Plays for the French Classroom	$21.95	
PG4	Mighty Mini-Plays for the German Classroom	$21.95	
PE4	Mighty Mini-Plays for the ESL Classroom	$21.95	
GT6	Get Them Talking!	$21.95	
SNLI/II	Sing 'n Learn Verbs in Spanish I or II price each	$21.95	
SS	Skinny Skits (in Spanish)	$24.95	
PPT	Petites Pièces de Théâtre	$24.95	
		Sub-Total	
	Shipping & Handling 10%, $5.00 minimum		
	Add 8.25% sales tax when applicable		
		Total	

Manner of Payment: Check_____   Charge _____   Purchase Order #_____

Name: _____
School: _____ District: _____
Address:_____
City: _____ State: _____ Zip Code: _____

Charge Card Information:

Cardholder Name _____
Street Address _____
City _____ State _____ Zip _____
Phone H: (_____) _____
Credit Card Number: (VISA or Mastercard Only)

Expiration Date ____/____/____ (include last 3 numbers on signature strip _____
NOTE: School districts, please enclose Purchase Order. Allow 2-3 weeks delivery.